D0616701

Miracles
Happen
When You Pray

Miracles
Happen
When You Pray

TRUE STORIES OF THE
REMARKABLE POWER OF PRAYER

Quin Sherrer

ZondervanPublishingHouse
Grand Rapids, Michigan

A Division of HarperCollinsPublishers

Miracles Happen When You Pray
Copyright © 1997 by Quin Sherrer

Requests for information should be addressed to:

ZondervanPublishingHouse
Grand Rapids, Michigan 49530

ISBN: 1-56865-385-9

All Scripture quotations, unless otherwise indicated, are taken from the *Holy Bible: New International Version*®. NIV®. Copyright © 1973, 1978, 1984 by International Bible Society. Used by permission of Zondervan Publishing House. All rights reserved.

Other versions are abbreviated as follows: KJV (King James Version), NKJV (New King James Version), LB (The Living Bible), NASB (New American Standard Bible)

In a few instances in this book, names of individuals and locations have been changed to protect the privacy of the individuals involved, at their request.

All rights reserved. No part of this publication may be reproduced, stored in a retrieval system, or transmitted in any form or by any means—electronic, mechanical, photocopy, recording, or any other—except for brief quotations in printed reviews, without the prior permission of the publisher.

Interior design by Sue Vandenberg Koppenol

Printed in the United States of America

We will tell the next generation
*the praiseworthy deeds of the L*ORD,
his power, and the wonders he has done . . .
which he commanded our forefathers
to teach their children,
so the next generation would know them,
even the children yet to be born,
and they in turn would tell their children.
Then they would put their trust in God
and would not forget his deeds.

PSALM 78:4B–7A

To my children
Quinett Rae, Keith Alan, Sherry Ruth
And to their children, my grandchildren
Kara Nicole
Evangeline Noel
Lyden Benjamin
Samuel Johannes
Victoria Jewett

CONTENTS

ACKNOWLEDGMENTS

I am thankful to God for the miracle of including me in his family.

I am grateful to my Zondervan editor, Ann Spangler, for her encouragement and expertise that made this book possible, and to Evelyn Bence and Verlyn Verbrugge, who polished it with their editorial pens.

To all those who shared their miracle stories in answer to prayer, a big thank you! So many sent me accounts of their miracles, it was impossible to include them all. Thank you, each and every one who wrote.

It is my prayer that those who read this book will be drawn closer to God and have more hope to believe for a miracle too.

PREFACE

Our God is a miracle-working God. Even a casual reading of the Bible reveals that miracles, signs, and wonders occurred in the early church as believers expected them and had faith to trust for them; just read the Gospels and the book of Acts.

Maybe you are saying, "That was then; what about now?" My purpose in this book is to show you that such things still happen. True, God may not always answer our prayers with a miracle. Yet miracles still *do* happen, often as the result of the prayers of ordinary men and women. God is still performing miracles in answer to the prayers of believers.

Miracles Happen When You Pray is a book for any of us who have ever longed for a miracle. In these pages I relate remarkable stories of men and women who have been healed from serious illness, protected from financial reverses, reunited with lost people and things, and rescued in life and death situations. These inspiring stories teach us much about prayer—about believing in God's love and accepting his will, about gratitude for his mercy, and about the nature of faith and trust. They are true stories of ordinary people who know the extraordinary power of a loving God.

In addition to recounting many wonderful stories, I hope to provide you with practical insights to encourage and motivate praying regularly and more effectively. Your faith will be strengthened, and you will learn some biblical principles to help you.

At the end of each section, I have included Scripture passages to bolster your faith and guide your intercession. I encourage you to make these verses from the Bible a part of your prayer arsenal.

I hope this book will inspire you while it motivates and encourages you to pray according to God's Spirit. Most of all I trust that you will discover a new depth of God's love and compassion for you, his child.

PART ONE

Praying for a Miracle

*He performs wonders that cannot be fathomed,
miracles that cannot be counted.*

JOB 5:9

Prayer is a powerful thing, for God has bound
and tied himself thereto. None can believe how
powerful prayer is, and what it is able to effect,
but those who have learned it by experience.

MARTIN LUTHER

*I*n all of us I sense a universal and instinctive longing for miracles.

We desire to see our own lives and the lives of those we love transformed by the touch of extraordinary grace.

God listens to our heart. He hears our whispered prayer. And somehow our prayers are tightly aligned to the granting of the miracles we long for. I see prayer as being a *catalyst* for miracles. As C. Peter Wagner has said, "[God] has made certain things He wishes to do in human affairs contingent on the prayers of His people."[1]

Maybe you are a doubter. Perhaps you do not think God would or could work a miracle for you. Hold on! He may have already performed a miracle in your life—a miracle you haven't recognized as such. By the time you have finished this book, I trust you will clearly recognize a few that have touched you.

God is still in the miracle-working, life-altering business. He is busily at work behind the scenes to help you fulfill his purpose for your life.

WHAT IS A MIRACLE?

What is a miracle? I have asked this question to groups at churches, colleges, and women's seminars across the country as I have spoken on my six previous books on prayer. Scores of men and women have told me personally or have written to me about their own miraculous answers to prayer. In answer to this question I have received a variety of answers.

- An unexplainable, unusual event
- A supernatural intervention when I needed it most
- God's divine protection when there was no way of escape
- An unaccountable healing that baffles even doctors

- A financial need met—a need that I could not handle without supernatural or divine intervention
- An answer to a deep, longing desire that no one else knew about
- A phenomenal event or happening; a work of wonder
- A divinely orchestrated appointment or meeting with someone I needed to see or know (what some would call an unlikely "chance meeting")
- An extraordinary circumstance through which I felt God's overwhelming love

A dictionary defines *miracle* as "an event that cannot be explained by the known laws of nature and is therefore attributed to divine intervention."[2] Jamie Buckingham wrote: "The bigger our concept of God, the more we see Him as the God of miracles. Miracles reveal the nature of God. Thus, there are no big miracles and little miracles. All miracles are big—for they reflect the nature of our big God."[3]

How do we get a miracle? *Miracles come by faith in God's existing power, not by a formula or a ritual we perform.* Jesus said that if you have faith even as small as a mustard seed, you can tell your mountain (obstacle, hindrance, problem) to move, and nothing will be impossible for you (see Matthew 17:20). A mustard seed is mighty tiny. To pray for miracles, you don't have to wait until you have big-big faith. Start with what you have now.

HOW DO I PRAY?

So how do you pray for a miracle?

Here is the starting point: Seek God regarding the situation that presents the need for a miracle. Ask, "Lord, what do you want in this circumstance?" Then *wait* on God for him to reveal his mind, his will, in the situation.

Seeking to know God's will calls us to read his Word, the Bible; we get acquainted with his character by studying that Word. For example, Scripture clearly states that it is not God's will that any perish (see 2 Peter 3:9). Knowing that, we can confidently pray for his arm of love to save those who are far from him. The Bible says there is a time to be born and a time to die (see Ecclesiastes 3:2). But God doesn't want us to die before our time. Some sicknesses and diseases we are to fight. And we resist them with faith and by quoting the Word of God—the Scriptures—asking God to show us appropriate passages for our situation.

To pray is to work in concert with God, not to use him as we wish. We don't demand. We come as children come to a parent, asking and believing that he has our best interest at heart. Prayer involves, then, a personal relationship with a heavenly Father through his Son, Jesus. It is our privilege to speak to him; we must then wait to listen to him.

It is important to recognize that prayer is not a way to manipulate God. "If it were," says C. Peter Wagner, "Christian prayer would not differ from magic or sorcery. Christian prayer brings us into such intimacy with God that we are able to tune in to His love, grace, will, purpose and timing and then adjust our own planning accordingly."[4]

ESSENTIAL PRAYER INGREDIENTS

I hate to admit it, but my early prayer life was more crisis-based than belief-based. When one of my children was headed to the emergency room, I would cry in a panic, "Lord, do something—because I can't." Other times I prayed what I would call "general bless us" prayers.

One evening at a writing conference, twenty-three years ago, I was seated across the dinner table from Catherine Marshall, whom I had long admired; I knew her reputation as an author and also as a praying mother. I asked her pointedly, "Can you give me some advice on how to pray more effectively for my three children?"

"Be as specific in your prayers as you can and plant waiting prayers for your children's future," she said. She had prayed specifically, she confided, for her son's future wife when he was still small. She called that "planting waiting prayers"—prayers that wouldn't be answered until some future date.

Later that evening she challenged us with a startling question: "When you pray, do you really expect anything to happen?"

I pondered that question: Did I really expect anything to happen when I prayed? Do you?

I began to dig through the Bible to read everything I could find on prayer. God, I discovered, is pleased with prayers of thanksgiving, petition, confession, praise, and intercession. Sometimes he wants us to fast while we pray. For more than twenty years now I have kept my own prayer diary, journaling God's faithful answers. I have watched him deal with each member of our family and gently bring three wandering youngsters back to himself.

Not that all my requests have been granted. But as I have developed a closer intimacy with the Lord, I have reveled in his love. I have learned that he wants the best for us, and now and then that calls for a miracle.

The following are some prayer keys I have found to be effective. Add yours to these.

Be explicit. Jesus told a parable about a man who wakes up his friend at midnight to ask for bread—explicitly three loaves—for his unexpected company (see Luke 11:5).

Be persistent. The man knocks continuously until his friend gets out of bed to answer his request. This isn't saying that prayers are needed to overcome God's reluctance to answer. Rather, this parable encourages us to be bold and persistent when we pray. Jesus said to ask, seek, knock— a continuous asking, seeking, knocking (see Luke 11:8–10).

Be in agreement. I usually ask a prayer partner (my husband, a close friend, or a prayer support team) to pray with me concerning a pressing need. Jesus gives a pattern for prayers of agreement (see Matthew 18:19–20). Many miracles related in this book came as a result of people praying together in unity for a healing, for protection, for provision, for intervention, for deliverance, and for other needs.

Be Bible-based. As we get better acquainted with the Bible, we grow to know God better and understand how to pray in accordance with his will. We come to know what he says about salvation, healing, deliverance, family values, the abundant life on earth, and heaven's promises. I often find a Bible verse I can turn into a prayer for my current need. David's psalms are a good place to start.

Be open to the Holy Spirit. After ascending to heaven, Jesus sent the Holy Spirit to help us pray what is on God's heart. Whatever our circumstance or crisis, when we invite the Holy Spirit to pray through us, we may find ourselves praying things we could never have "thought up" (see Romans 8:26–27).

Never presume God is going to answer in your preconceived way or exact time frame. I have had to learn the difference between presumption and faith. Presumption means assuming God will answer me in the exact way I envision and in my timetable. I have attempted to "box God in" by my selfish expectations. Faith, on the other hand, is a supernatural ability to trust God when he has spoken to my heart—trusting him to fulfill his will in his time and in his way. Often this "inner trust" or faith level comes after time spent in prayer, listening and waiting on him.

Be thankful. Present prayer requests to God with thanksgiving, thanking him *in advance* for answering your prayer—his way (see Philippians 4:6).

Be willing to fast. Those serious enough to abstain voluntarily from food have found that fasting and prayer often yield one or more of these results: directions and answers from God, a deeper understanding of Scripture, a closer walk with God, a humbling of oneself, a healing, or even a deliverance.

Praise God. He is enthroned in the praises of his people (see Psalm 22:3). Whenever we as God's people praise him, we put ourselves in a position to receive his blessings because our focus is on him, not our need. Psalm 22 affirms God's goodness while asking for his presence.

Trust him—always. When we come to the end of ourselves, we can still praise him. We can admit: "We have no power ... [nor do we] know what to do, but our eyes are upon you" (2 Chronicles 20:12). We don't know *how* or *when* our miracle is coming, but we praise him for his lovingkindness and mercy. We never give up on expecting our miracle!

HINDRANCES TO PRAYER

Three of the greatest hindrances to answered prayer are unbelief, unforgiveness, and unconfessed sin.

Jesus addresses the first two in Mark 11:24–25: "Therefore I tell you, whatever you ask for in prayer, believe that you have received it, and it will be yours. And when you stand praying, if you hold anything against anyone, forgive him, so that your Father in heaven may forgive you your sins." It is a twofold condition: to believe that God hears and to forgive.

At the beginning of any prayer time, it is helpful to confess any unforgiveness, judgmental attitude, hatred, disappointment, unbelief, or anything that is displeasing to God. Give him the "junk" that you have allowed to plug up your pipeline of communication with him. With the lines of communication open, expect to receive an answer to your prayer.

LESSONS FROM A GOSPEL MIRACLE

Before I relate a number of miracles—some "big," some "little"—that are answers to prayers, let me review a few lessons about prayer and miracles that I have drawn from one of my favorite biblical miracles, a healing recounted by Luke, the physician gospel writer.

When a blind beggar in Jericho heard that Jesus of Nazareth was passing by, he yelled, "Jesus, have mercy on me." People around him tried to make him be quiet, but he cried out all the more.

> Jesus stopped ... [and] asked him. "What do you want me to do for you?"
> "Lord, I want to see," he replied.
> Jesus said to him, "Receive your sight; your faith has healed you."

Luke goes on to say that the man immediately received his sight, followed Jesus, and praised God; the people observing the miracle also praised God (see Luke 18:35–42). This miracle illustrates:

- The man in need was *specific in asking*. (He wanted to see and was persistent in crying out for mercy.)
- Jesus told him to "receive" his sight. The miracle was immediate.
- Jesus commended his faith. The blind beggar did not let others stop him from reaching the Miracle-Worker. He believed that if he could get to Jesus, he would be healed.
- When he was healed, he followed Jesus.
- His healing caused all the people who witnessed it to praise God. This crowd had first discouraged the blind man from reaching Jesus. Now that he was healed, the focus was not on the beggar but on God, from whom the miracle came.

As we seek out and act on our faith in the Miracle-Worker, we too are to be specific in our requests, persistent in our prayers, and receptive to God's Word. We must not allow others to discourage us; and when our miracle comes, we must give God the credit.

The Bible is full of God's miraculous action on behalf of his people—Daniel rescued from the lions' den; Joseph plucked from prison to become prime minister of Egypt; the Israelites, led by Moses, rescued from Pharaoh's cruel dictatorship through the miraculous opening of the Red Sea. All these were praying men!

Jesus healed the sick, cast out demons, raised the dead, and fed the multitudes. After three years of teaching his disciples, he embraced the cross. No miracle is more significant than Christ's resurrection.

And God is still working astounding miracles.

The following true stories illustrate the power of prayer and the power of our great miracle-working God. As you read these accounts, praise his name. Trust God for a miracle of your own.

A NIGHT OF TERROR

One evening in August 1991 Carol and Dick Brown sat in the family room of their Seattle home, watching the late news. They had no reason to think they were not safe and secure, but then it happened.

An intruder peering out through the tight veil of a nylon stocking burst into the room. Waving a handgun and brandishing a knife, he shouted, "Give me all your money. I want money. I want it now. I'm sick. I'm really sick. . . ." This was the voice of a desperate man. They sensed he might kill if he weren't taken seriously.

The man demanded that Dick hand over his diamond ring, the heirloom handed down to Dick by his grandfather.

Carol's heart raced, her old enemy fear welling up, trying to overtake her.

Again the man yelled for cash. "Give me money. Now."

Their money, they explained, was in Dick's wallet, upstairs in the master bedroom.

Like a drill sergeant—a jittery drill sergeant—he barked out instructions. "We will all go up there and get it." He aimed the gun at their heads and marched them upstairs. Carol quickly replayed the day in her mind. *Had she forgotten to lock the back door after cleaning up from their backyard barbecue?*

She remembered her morning devotional reading, Psalm 91. She had meditated particularly on verses 9–10: "If you make the Most High your dwelling—even the LORD, who is my refuge—then no harm will befall you, no disaster will come near your tent." She had admitted her cowardice to the Lord, even taking the time to write in her prayer journal, "Lord, I'm such a chicken. I don't want to live in fear."

And now this. Once in the bedroom, the intruder opened the wallet and found only eight dollars. Furious, he cursed loudly.

Carol suddenly remembered the gold coins she had uncovered just the day before when rearranging Dick's bureau drawers. Maybe they would satisfy the intense man and make him leave. She spoke up: "You can have our gold coins—in one of those drawers." She pointed to the bureau.

Still holding a gun on them, the man dropped to his knees and pawed through the drawers.

All the time Carol prayed silently, calling on the name of the Lord. *Jesus, help us. Jesus. Jesus. Jesus.*

When the man found the coins, Carol felt a surge of strength, boldness, courage lunging up within her. Looking straight at him, she spoke out, her voice slightly raised, "In the name of Jesus, this is *our* house!"

The results were immediate. "I didn't want to hurt you. I didn't want to hurt you," he whimpered apologetically. Still on his knees, he fell over to his side as if a giant hand had shoved him.

Stumbling up, he ran out the door, down the stairs, and out into the night.

Carol didn't know who was more surprised, she or the fleeing man. She, who had been a coward, had suddenly been emboldened to declare her property off-limits to an intruder.

Carol had previously had a "head knowledge" of Jesus' promise to believers: "I have given you authority . . . to overcome all the power of the enemy; nothing will harm you" (Luke 10:19). But now she was able to claim it as true in her own experience.

By simply speaking the name of Jesus, her courage increased, her fear dissipated. And the Lord, who was her refuge, kept danger away from her home. It was a watershed moment for Carol; the grip of fear was broken from her forever. She no longer lives in fear.

A new boldness in Christ is a common result of miracles—even miracles sent in response to a short, powerful prayer: "Jesus, help!"

A LITTLE NAP-TIME MIRACLE

Kim Finley, a homemaker, praises God for his hand of divine protection when . . . it might have been otherwise.

Kim had just put her two daughters, three-year-old Molly and one-year-old Sarah, down to nap in the bedroom they shared. Kim was hoping for a few restful minutes to herself.

But shortly she heard a momentous boom—a crash in the girls' bedroom. Molly came running out, yelling, "Something's happened—something's happened to Sarah!"

"O Lord, help us." That was all Kim could think to pray as she rushed to her daughter. She prayed often, asking God to protect her family. He knew her desperate need, she was sure.

When she reached the bedroom she found a tall, eight-drawer, solid maple dresser turned over flat on the floor. Her baby wasn't in her bed. Could she be buried under the dresser? Obviously the girls had been playing instead of napping.

Trying to stay calm and rational, Kim quickly started calculating a disaster plan: Which was the quickest route to the hospital? Should she call 911 first or just go?

Kim swiftly hoisted the heavy dresser from the top. Then she saw her baby, face down with her arms next to her face, lying underneath where the dresser had fallen. As Kim continued to lift the bureau, drawers started tumbling out, some right on top of Sarah. Kim desperately yanked them away, and then her eyes met Sarah's. She held out her arms to her mommy but never cried.

Molly, who had accidently toppled the dresser when climbing onto it to get something down, screamed and screamed. Kim hugged her daughters close to her, praising God that they both had been spared injury! Just a little miracle at nap time in answer to a quick, desperate prayer that followed several years of daily intercession for her family.

PEACE TO DISTURBED STUDENTS

Barbara Graham knew the situation on her job called for supernatural intervention. God's peace was sorely needed, and prayer was the avenue that would make it possible.

Barbara tells her story:

I work for the school transportation department as a substitute attendant on the special education buses. One week I was assigned to a bus transporting young adults aged fifteen to seventeen to a hospital that serves as a tight-security school. These kids couldn't attend public school because they were violent and harmful to themselves and others.

The first young man we picked up was so violent that a trained technician from the hospital rode along with him. He was separated from the others on the bus, and under no circumstances was he to be left alone. I was anxious about this assignment, wondering how I could hold up over a period of days. The previous attendant had been stabbed, and another had been bitten by a six-foot, hundred-and-eighty-pound boy. Anything could, and did, set them off. On our morning route three boys jumped another boy. I was so glad when we reached the hospital.

To tell the truth, I didn't want to go back in the afternoon to take them home. But I prayed, and a Scripture came to mind: "I am sending you out like sheep among wolves. Therefore be as shrewd as snakes and as innocent as doves" (Matthew 10:16). I went back to work early so I could pray over the bus—door, windows, and each seat. I prayed for calm, peace, and cooperation. When our bus driver arrived, I told her I had prayed that each student would have peace.

We arrived at the hospital grounds and loaded the students on the bus. Even before we pulled out, the most violent student fell asleep. Ten minutes later, another was asleep. Twenty minutes, thirty, fifty—more than an hour later there was still not a sound on the bus from any of them. No one seemed to move. There was definitely peace and calm, all right.

The driver was amazed. "They . . . they . . . were good!" she stammered. Both of us were grateful for an answered prayer. It may not be the greatest miracle God ever performed, but it was the miracle we needed that day.

The students traveled in peace and so did Barbara and the bus driver, enabling them to arrive safely. Sometimes God gives us just the miracle we need for the moment—in answer to prayer.

CORRIE'S PRISON MIRACLE

During World War II Betsie ten Boom died in a Nazi prison camp. She and her sister, Corrie, had been sent there because they had been caught hiding Jews in their Dutch home. Years after the war, Corrie wrote about an answer to prayer regarding a seemingly insignificant item. Betsie's specific prayer and mustard-seed faith is still an inspiration. In her words:

> I will tell you something that happened when I was a prisoner in a concentration camp with my sister, Betsie. One morning I had a terrible cold, and I said to Betsie, "What can I do? I have no handkerchief."
>
> "Pray," she said. I smiled, but she prayed, "Father, Corrie has got a cold, and she has no handkerchief. Will you give her one in Jesus' name, Amen."
>
> I could not help laughing, but as she said "Amen," I heard my name called. I went to the window, and there stood my friend who worked in the prison hospital.
>
> "Quickly, quickly! Take this little package; it is a little present for you." I opened the package, and inside was a handkerchief.
>
> "Why in the world did you bring me this? Did I ask you for it? Did you know that I have a cold?"
>
> "No, but I was folding handkerchiefs in the hospital, and a voice in my heart said, 'Take one to Corrie ten Boom.'"
>
> What a miracle! Can you understand what that handkerchief told me at that moment? It told me that in heaven there is a loving Father who hears when one of his children on this very small planet asks for an impossible little thing—a handkerchief. And that heavenly Father tells one of his other children to take one to Corrie ten Boom.
>
> God answers prayers, and God's promises are a greater reality than our problems.[5]

SMALL REQUEST: BIG GOD

Susie Lynn's friend gave her a special piece of jewelry—a blue topaz ring set in sterling silver. Unfortunately, she lost it. Where? When? How? She didn't know. For the next nine years she hoped it would be found. From time to time she would pray about that ring. Each year during spring house cleaning, she would search for it—again.

But it never showed up. Then one spring day while in the shower, Susie reminded God that she would like to have her topaz jewelry back. Her request was heartfelt and specific.

Three days later her dad and brother were plowing up an old flower bed for her mom. Suddenly they hit something hard, and, though tarnished, the silver reflected in the sunlight. They picked it up to find that it was Susie's lost jewelry. "What a miracle!" she shouted, when her mother, wearing the ring on her own little finger, broke the surprise to her.

That was two years ago, and to this day she praises God for his care of the little things in our lives. Whenever someone admires Susie's topaz, she tells the lost-and-found story, using the opportunity to tell someone about God's caring power.

HER OWN PRIVATE PILOT

Linelle Kelly tells how she felt God's overwhelming love through an answer to prayer and a long-held heart's desire.

After retiring from the Air Force, my brother Roger took a job as a pilot for a major airline. He lives in Spokane, Washington, and I live near Omaha, Nebraska. We don't see each other much.

One day I told the Lord, "It would be really fun to walk on a plane someday and find that Roger was the pilot." I prayed it only once, but then I tucked the desire away in my heart.

Several years later I was flying to the West Coast. It was my first time flying alone. As I boarded the plane in Omaha, a voice inside me said, "Look in the cockpit." I turned my head and there was Roger.

When I called his name, he swung around in his chair. He looked at me and was even more startled than I. We hugged each other—like an old fashioned reunion.

Over the intercom Roger announced that his sister was on board, and I felt like royalty.

"Flying on the same plane with your brother is a real coincidence," one of the flight attendants told me. I said it wasn't just coincidence, but God had done it in answer to a prayer of mine.

Roger and I both had layover time in Denver, so we had a chance to spend some fun time together, a rarity for us. God does give us the desires of our hearts.

Linelle's story reminds me of one of the definitions of *miracle* mentioned earlier in the chapter—an extraordinary circumstance through which I felt God's overwhelming love. He knows the desires of our hearts. As hymn writer James Montgomery has said, "Prayer is the soul's sincere desire."

FASTING AND PRAYER PAY OFF

Carolyn Rudolph believes that her fasting and prayer helped save her daughter from making one of the biggest mistakes of her life. She tells her story:

The day our daughter turned thirteen was the day she began to rebel against our authority. Laura wanted more than anything to be accepted by her classmates and friends. But it was a case of the blind leading the blind. She was dating a sixteen-year-old who smoked, drank, did drugs, and was sexually active. He lived with his twenty-four-year-old uncle, who was later arrested for a sexual assault.

Of course we were terribly concerned. As Christian parents we hadn't expected her to make such friends. (Maybe we were a little naive.) When we learned her boyfriend had talked Laura into running away with him, possibly the coming weekend, my husband and I knew we had to do something.

So we began to fast and pray. Every night that week one of us stayed awake. We took shifts, guarding the telephone, making sure she was in her bedroom, and praying for her safety and protection from those luring temptations. We cried out to God on her behalf. We continued our fasting and prayer through that weekend. When Monday morning came and she was still living under our roof, we were so relieved and grateful to God.

Then it was as if God swooped down and came to the rescue. The boyfriend's mother came to town, withdrew him from school, and moved him back into her home many miles away. My husband and I thanked God that our daughter would no longer be under the influence of this young man.

That was years ago. Laura is now a grown woman, happily married to what Carolyn calls "a good man."

Fasting and prayer paid off, as these parents interceded for a miracle in their daughter's life—and today Laura is still grateful for praying parents.

GIVE AWAY WHAT YOU HAVE?

What do you do when the pantry is empty? You might learn a lesson from Polly and David Simpchen—who needed a miracle.

David and Polly were expecting their first baby within the week, and times were particularly hard. David had been working, spraying ceilings for a small dry-wall company. He had not had any work that week, however, and the two of them were living hand to mouth. For the first time in their short married life, their food supply was down to nothing. They had no milk, no bread, no peanut butter.

In the refrigerator was just enough hamburger to make one patty. The cupboard contained a can of vegetable soup, a little flour, and a bit of sugar—all they had left.

That Sunday morning David prayed specifically for God to provide money for rent, food, and gas. They then went to church, grateful they would at least be eating lunch with friends. In the afternoon as Polly was resting, she heard a knock at her door. She answered, seeing an unusually tall grey-haired woman. "I am hungry," she said. That's all—no further explanations.

"Come in and I will fix you a hamburger and some soup," Polly volunteered eagerly. She had never had such a request, but she wasn't going to let anyone go hungry!

"No, just give me the hamburger meat," the woman said. "I'll wait here."

Polly went to the refrigerator, ready to relinquish her last bit of meat. She silently prayed again her husband's prayer—that God would supply their needs. In faith that her prayer would be answered, she handed the woman the tiny portion of ground meat, all she had. The mysterious woman thanked her, turned, and left. Polly called David quickly to tell him what happened. They both looked out the window, expecting to see her walking down the sidewalk.

But she was gone. They ran out into the yard. Polly went to the left, David to the right. They looked everywhere for her. But she had disappeared. They were puzzled.

The next morning on their front porch they found an envelope with a check and a note from some neighbors. It was enough to cover their rent, some food, and gas for the car.

Polly saw a glimpse of God's graceful plan that is often beyond our imagination. He had given her the gift of faith to believe he would take care of their needs, even if she gave away their last portion of meat to a stranger. And he had honored her generosity.

Polly's story reminds me of the story about the generous widow blessed by God through Elijah. I'll recap that biblical story and many inspiring contemporary true stories in the next part—"Miracles of Provision."

Remember, miracles happen when we pray—when we seek God, get to know him, and live lives of faith.

Praying the Scriptures

MIRACLES HAPPEN WHEN WE PRAY

I have selected the following passages from Scripture to help bolster your faith and enable you to pray more effectively. Try making these a regular part of your prayer life.

Again, I [Jesus] tell you that if two of you on earth agree about anything you ask for, it will be done for you by my Father in heaven. For where two or three come together in my name, there am I with them.

MATTHEW 18:19–20

Jesus answered . . . "The miracles I do in my Father's name speak for me. . . . My sheep listen to my voice: I know them, and they follow me. I will give them eternal life, and they shall never perish. . . ."

JOHN 10:25–28A

[Paul wrote]: The things that mark an apostle—signs, wonders and miracles—were done among you with great perseverance.

2 CORINTHIANS 12:12

[The early Christians prayed]: "Now, Lord, . . . stretch out your hand to heal and perform miraculous signs and wonders through the name of your holy servant Jesus."

ACTS 4:29–30

Our Father in heaven, hallowed be your name, your kingdom come, your will be done on earth as it is in heaven.

MATTHEW 6: 9–10

PART TWO

Miracles of Provision

And my God will meet all your needs according to his glorious riches in Christ Jesus.

PHILIPPIANS 4:19

The promises of God are just as good as ready money any day.

BILLY BRAY

One of my favorite biblical miracles is a story about God graciously providing physical sustenance to a desperately poor woman, known as the widow of Zarephath.

During a severe drought, the traveling prophet Elijah asked this woman for water and a piece of bread. The widow admitted that she had only enough flour and oil to make one meal for her son and herself; they would eat it and then die. Elijah listened but then instructed her to "make a small cake of bread from what you have and bring it to me, and then make something for yourself and your son. For this is what the LORD, the God of Israel says, 'The jar of flour will not be used up and the jug of oil will not run dry until the day the LORD gives rain on the land'" (1 Kings 17:13–14). The widow did as Elijah told her, and her flour and oil miraculously lasted—replenished itself— until the end of the long famine.

This miracle took place several thousand years ago. It still bolsters the faith of God's people. You and I both know that God's children, now as then, sometimes find themselves in financial binds where the only way out may be a God-sent miracle.

We may have suffered a financial setback without having been disobedient or careless. At other times our unwise or wrong choices may have plunged us into hot water. Admittedly, some of us are irresponsible, begging God to bail us out time and time again; yet we are unwilling to exercise self-control in our spending.

Or maybe we are unwilling to give the firstfruits of our labor to him. "I gave God my business, then I never gave him anything from it, and I wondered why I went bankrupt!" one man told me. He is prospering now, he says, because he began giving ten percent of his earnings to God's work. He bases this claim on a biblical principle that says when we bring tithes and offerings to the Lord, he will open the floodgates of heaven and pour out blessings (see Malachi 3:8–10).

If I consider everything I have as belonging to the Lord, then I give my needs to him and trust him for their provision. We are often tempted to believe that "it is all up to us" when it comes to providing finances for ourselves. Of course, it is wise to prepare for the future. But if we are doing what we sincerely believe God wants us to do, then anxiety is not in order.

Remember Paul's promise to the Philippian believers: "And my God will meet all your needs according to his glorious riches in Christ Jesus" (Philippians 4:19). Note the noun here—*needs*. It helps to distinguish between a need and a want. God meets our needs, but not necessarily all our wants. God miraculously kept the Israelites alive forty years in the desert by providing manna from heaven, but they murmured and complained. They wanted something more delectable to eat.

I am not saying that tithing is a magic formula. Nor am I implying that if we just live according to God's will, we won't have financial setbacks. What a distortion of the truth that would be! Indeed, we can allow such setbacks to focus our attention on God's deeper purpose. Is there something he wants us to learn? We trust God, not a particular outcome. And the Lord will not be outdone in generosity.

Many of us do not want to admit we are beholden to anybody—even to a power greater than ourselves. But the truth is, we are dependent on God. He is the Creator, we are the created. God yearns for us to express our gratitude. The Psalms are full of thankfulness. I like the ones that say, "His love endures forever." When we are specific in our thanksgiving to him, power is released.

I turn now to a number of modern-day miracles of provision. May these stories so build your faith, that even if you have made some financial blunders, you can ask God for his grace and forgiveness and trust him for a turnaround in your life.

I'LL TAKE THAT ONE, LORD

What would you do if you had needs but no money to meet them? Annette Smith found out how God can provide for a widow in ways that do not necessarily involve cold cash.

Newly widowed, Annette was overwhelmed on several fronts. Financially, she was trying to pay off medical bills. As a homeowner, there was property to manage. When spring came, she started thinking about selling the house— surrounded by two acres of lawn. She faced a major problem: The lawnmowers no longer worked.

One weekend, as she got ready to go to her Mom's for a visit, she took another look at the weeds and grass—or was it a hayfield?

"God, if you want this mowed, okay. But if not, I'll praise you anyway," she said as she drove off.

When she returned home, she couldn't believe her eyes. The entire two acres had been beautifully manicured. Two friends admitted they had hand-mowed it.

Annette was exuberantly grateful, and yet she faced reality: The grass would grow back and continue to need mowing.

Without a husband, she depended on God for everything, talking to him just as she had formerly talked to her husband, Gene. "Lord, I know I need to be specific when I ask for something. . . ." Flipping through the current Sears catalog, she stopped at a page picturing a beautiful self-starter tractor mower that cost one thousand dollars. "That one will do, God. Thanks."

Then she noticed a hand-mower she would also need to reach around the edges. "And that one too, God," she said, placing her finger on the catalog picture. She certainly did not have the money for such expensive equipment. But Annette left her request where she had put it—in God's hands.

Later that spring a Sears truck drove up, and the delivery man said, "Here's your order."

"I didn't order anything from Sears."

"Are you Annette Smith?"

"Yes."

"Then these are yours," he said, as he unloaded his cargo—the exact self-starter tractor mower she had seen and prayed for. Then he brought out a hand-mower—the very one she had pointed to in the catalog. Finally, he unloaded an electric trimmer for weeds—a bonus she hadn't requested.

Annette later discovered the identity of her benefactor. A friend of Gene's had felt the Lord say to him, "When you sell that motorcycle, buy Annette Smith a tractor mower and a hand-mower." He had figured they would cost a certain amount, but when he went to buy them, he had enough money left over to get the electric trimmer.

Annette gladly accepted God's provision through a friend. But to her it was a miraculous answer to her specific prayer.

If God was that concerned about a Wisconsin widow and her grass, isn't he just as concerned about you and your personal needs? Of course he is! Her story encourages us to pray specifically for the things we need—and to wait expectantly for one of God's surprises.

WATER WELL MIRACLE

When Marine Major General Charles Krulak needed a miracle of water for troops about to lead an attack on Iraq during the 1991 war in the Persian Gulf, he did what he always did—he prayed.

He had been assigned to prepare supplies for the frontal attack by allied forces against Iraqi troops. Because of a threat of chemical warfare, lots of water would be needed for the decontamination process.

He thought he was ready, having dug water wells that could supply one hundred thousand gallons a day for the ground offensive.

Then General Norman Schwarzkopf's strategy changed as the Iraqis dug in. General Krulak's operation was to move to a flat area called "gravel plains," seventy-four miles to the northwest.

As they dug for water there, only desert dust came out. The general consulted oil company engineers and Saudi bedouins. Still no water—only dry holes.

General Krulak prayed every day for a solution to the water problem as well as for the war effort. Ever since 1977 he had made it a practice to pray at 7:15 each morning. Staff members were invited to join him. The anticipated ground attack was only a few days away. One morning a colonel interrupted their prayer meeting to ask the general to accompany him somewhere. He had discovered something but he wouldn't say what. He wanted the general to see for himself.

As they traveled down a road built by the Marine Corps, they saw what looked like a pipe sticking out of the ground about fifty meters off the road. A bar protruding from the pipe formed a cross. Then the general saw at the base of the pipe a newly painted red pump, a green diesel generator, four new batteries still wrapped in plastic, and one thousand gallons of diesel fuel stored in a tank above the ground.

All the equipment was new, and everything seemed ready to operate—except there was no key to start the generator. The general looked at his officer and said, "God did not put this here for us to be defeated for lack of a key."

Amazingly, when General Krulak pushed the starter, the new German-made generator purred and water began to flow. The well flowed within ten gallons of the one hundred thousand a day needed for the assault.

The general had traveled down that road many times, as had a division of men, some twenty thousand troops. No one had reported seeing that pipe.

General Krulak believes the well appeared as an answer to prayer. "There was no way anyone could have driven down that road and not seen that well and equipment painted in multiple colors. The United States Forces did not use diesel fuel; therefore, I believe the Lord provided fuel we did not have," he said.

Others thought the Saudis may have put the well there. "Even if the well had already been there, its discovery came at exactly the right time," General Krulak said.

With the water problem solved, military experts still predicted heavy casualties. Krulak believes God performed yet another miracle in answer to prayer. On February 24, just fifteen minutes before the 4 A.M. ground attack, the wind shifted, blowing from the southwest to northeast. Winds always blow in the same direction in that part of the country, Krulak said.

This change of wind neutralized the threat of poison gas, which now would have blown back toward the Iraqis. The wind changed back to its normal direction on February 28, within minutes of General Schwarzkopf's cease-fire order.

"That," declares Krulak, now the Commandant of the United States Marine Corps, "is the power of prayer."[1]

One could call it a double miracle in the middle of a war.

RIGHT ON TIME

Some miracles provide for our financial need and are so timely that they indicate God's direction for our lives. This was true for Dr. Harold Reents, who prayed a specific prayer several years ago when his vocational path seemed unclear.

My wife and I were in Australia, building a Bible school. Nothing seemed to be going right. We had run out of money. Things were so tight that year that we "had no Christmas." In our whole marriage, this rarely happened, but at this point both of us were "down" at the same time.

I had previously worked at a Bible school in the U.S., and a friend in the personnel department there had contacted me and asked me to return. My wife and I prayed together and agreed that if God did not provide $10,000 (U.S.) by January 22, we would return home. Maybe we had missed the Lord's direction in coming to Australia.

On January 22, at 10:00 P.M., we phoned our friend Al in the States to tell him we were returning. Before I could tell him our decision, Al told me to hang up; he would call us back—to save us the expense. I obliged and hung up.

Five seconds later the phone rang. I answered and blurted, "Al, that was the fastest return call I ever had."

The caller said, "This is not Al. I am from Singapore, and I have a prayer group that meets in my house on Fridays. We understand you are starting a Bible school. We would like to send you a love gift for the school."

When I hung up, I asked my wife, "What is God doing? Maybe we had better not be so hasty about leaving."

A minute later Al called from the States. He had been trying to get me on the phone, but, of course, the line had been busy. I quickly told him I could not commit to returning to the States until I was sure what God wanted.

Three days later a man came and handed me a check for $11,137 and some odd cents in Australian money. I went to the bank, and that day it was worth $10,000 in U.S. currency—not a penny less or a penny more.

We stayed and helped build the Bible school and a church. The miracle we experienced convinced us that God's provision is always right on time.

HER DREAM COMES TRUE

As a child Pam McKinney hoped someday to see for herself the places where Jesus walked, Paul taught, and Peter preached. As the years passed, she wondered if her dream to visit the Holy Land would ever be possible. And yet she often prayed for her miracle trip.

Finally, in November of 1994, she signed up for a trip to Israel. She did this as a grand leap of faith. You see, she did not have the money for the trip, not even the $200 deposit due at the end of the month.

As Pam prayed for the deposit money and planned toward the January trip to Israel, she decided to do a little background research on the land. What was the climate like? The terrain? What sights would she see? She only knew from reading the Bible and imagining the scenery. She pulled out the appropriate volume of the encyclopedia that had been packed away seven years, given to her by her mother-in-law. She opened the book and thumbed her way through the pages until she found what she was looking for—and more than she was looking for. Pressed between the pages beside a photo of Israel were crisp dollar bills. A total of $290! Was this her miracle? But she had asked for the $200 deposit. Why was there $290?

Because the books had been given to her secondhand, she felt she should call her mother-in-law and tell her about the "find." Was the money hers? What did she want Pam to do? Pam was overjoyed at her mother-in-law's reaction. She had been praying for $90 for a real estate course she wanted to take. Pam could keep the remaining $200 to use as a deposit on her trip.

Pam was so excited, she nearly forgot she still needed money for the rest of the trip. The surprise "Israel bills" seemed to be a confirmation that she should prepare to go. And the trip was further confirmed when, not long after, the owner of a consignment shop that Pam frequented offered her a temporary job. "That's how I earned money for my trip, and what a blessing that journey was," Pam told me.

By the way, her part-time job became permanent, and she still works at the consignment store—a job she loves. Some miracles of provision are not about *needs* but may be about long-prayed-for dreams.

A VISION IN AN AMBULANCE

Sometimes God's provision for the hour is his peace. Will Williamson discovered this one day far from home, strapped down to an ambulance stretcher.

Will relates his extraordinary experience:

In the spring of 1991 I was in Port Arthur, Texas, on business. Staying in a motel, I couldn't sleep for the discomfort in my chest. A year earlier I had suffered a mild heart attack, so I was worried. In the morning I called my wife, Tee. She consulted with my doctor and called me back. "Go to the nearest hospital. Tell them you had heart trouble last year. Don't even try to make it home."

At the hospital I remember thinking, "I can't be laid up in bed as an invalid. . . . I'm not afraid to die because I'll see Jesus and be with him. But have I left things in order for Tee? Will she have enough income to live on? What about the kids?"

I was checked into a hospital room, and they started running their tests. That afternoon the cardiologist said that because of my previous heart attack I should have an angiogram done. He described the "simple procedure."

I listened and thought, "I'm the one who gets a wire pushed up through my artery. That doesn't sound too simple to me." I didn't give him an immediate go ahead. Rather, I told him I was waiting for my wife. "We have to think and pray about such a decision."

The next morning Tee arrived from Aledo, Texas, near Fort Worth, a drive of some eight hours. I knew she had been praying. Once at my bedside she phoned several of our prayer partners, asking them to pray for my health and for guidance. To have the test or not—it was not an easy decision. We did not know this medical team, nor did we have the spiritual and emotional support we enjoyed at home. But the doctor advised against flying home until more tests were run, and so we were leaning toward giving our approval for the test. Things were further complicated by the fact that this hospital did not have the angiogram equipment. I would have to transfer to a different facility.

My luggage had been brought from the motel to my hospital room and stacked in a corner. I had a big heavy suitcase, a large suit bag, and a carry-on briefcase—a formidable load for my wife to handle by herself.

Then came the first of God's provisions for me. A man stood at the foot of my bed, talking to me. "Are you the one who needs some suitcases moved?" He was dressed in the white uniform of a hospital orderly. He was an enormous fellow with the brightest, widest grin on his face. His teeth glistened like ivory. He had huge arms and hands and his eyes sparkled. It was just like the stories I have read about angels, only then I wasn't thinking angels.

"I sure am," I said.

"Well, I'm here to help you move some suitcases. Where do they go?" he asked.

Tee explained where our truck was parked and pointed to the suitcases.

Then he looked at me with that wide smile, "What you got wrong with you? What are they going to do to you?"

"I think I'm going to have an angiogram done."

"You ever had one before?"

"Never," I answered.

"Well, let me tell you, I had one not too long ago. I was so scared, I cried. I held on to the nurse's hand so hard on the way to take the test. But there ain't nothing to it."

"Easy for you to say," I thought. "You are through it. I still have it ahead of me."

"Once I got on that table and they started, there wasn't nothing to it," he continued. "They didn't find anything wrong with me. I'm fine. Jesus took care of me. Here, let me get that baggage."

The test was "on," scheduled for later that afternoon. Despite this man's encouragement, a seed of doubt tried to take root in my mind. "Maybe you won't survive. Maybe you have something seriously wrong with your heart." I kept those thoughts at bay by praying and by reading a book about a great Christian intercessor.

The ambulance crew came to transfer me across town. I was still hooked up to an IV drip and connected to a heart monitor. Inside the ambulance, I was strapped on a stretcher fastened to the floor. Beside me was a long, vinyl bench. Usually an attendant sat on the bench, but this time he sat up front with the driver, leaving the bench empty. More probably, it was to set the scene for God's second provision.

I was resting comfortably, praying about the test. I laid my book on my chest and closed my eyes for just a moment. When I opened them, I glanced to my left and saw a figure dressed in a long dust-colored robe seated on the bench. He had shoulder-length light brown hair. Leaning forward slightly with his right arm resting on his right thigh, he looked straight ahead. I looked at him, but quickly turned away. I didn't comprehend what I was seeing. I looked a second time and turned away. In fact, at first I thought I was just seeing "something." The third time I looked I realized who was seated beside me. "It's Jesus," I said to myself. "That's Jesus sitting there."

At that very instant he spoke to me in a clear, kind voice. "Everything is going to be all right," he said. I closed my eyes, and when I opened them again, he was gone.

"That was Jesus," I said to myself again. "That was not a dream or an hallucination—that was Jesus." Immediately the nagging doubts and uncertainties were gone. I was at perfect peace, with a new frame of mind: "Let's get this test over. I'm ready to go home." God's second provision had come to take away my fears.

All the way to the hospital I rode in that peace. Even while I waited an hour for the lab I rested, thinking about Jesus and his ministering words. Eventually I was wheeled down to the lab. The doctor walked in, the lights were dimmed, the incision was made in my thigh, and the test began.

On the overhead television screen I could see the catheter wire worm its way up the artery toward my heart. Soon the doctor smiled. "I don't see any blockage." My attack had not been related to my heart after all. The diagnosis was peptic ulcer disease, treatable with medication. Tee and I made plans to drive home.

Several months after my encounter with Jesus in the ambulance, I was reading my Bible. In Revelation 1:13b–16, Jesus is described in these words:

> "like a son of man," dressed in a robe reaching down to his feet and with a golden sash around his chest. His head and hair were white like wool, as white as snow, and his eyes were like blazing fire. His feet were like bronze glowing in a furnace, and his voice was like the sound of rushing waters. In his right hand he held seven stars, and out of his mouth came a sharp double-edged sword. His face was like the sun shining in all its brilliance.

As I read those words I remembered the dust-colored robe Jesus had worn in the ambulance. There had not been a shining glory about him. His presence was not like the description I read in these verses. It puzzled me. I prayed. "Lord, you didn't look like that when you appeared to me in the ambulance."

Immediately he spoke to my heart and said, "I didn't come to you as your conquering king. I came to you as your friend." He'd been my provision all along.

Will's provision came in natural ways—from a man who not only moved his luggage but also encouraged him about the upcoming test—and in supernatural ways, by his visitation of Jesus in the ambulance. God knows exactly what provision we need at the moment we are praying for our miracle.

GOD CAN FIND CARS TOO

Have you ever been tempted to buy beyond your means? Sandra Wilkins and her husband, Frank, were in that predicament after the engine on their car blew up. They knew they had to replace the vehicle.

Sandra tells her story:

The agent who assessed the damage gave us a check for $2,750 in exchange for what was left of the car. Check in hand, Frank and I set off car hunting.

On an extremely hot day in July, we test-drove used car after used car. Most were losers—foul odors, broken air conditioners, and the like. I kept praying I would not say something that might provoke an argument with my husband. It wasn't easy when he would make positive comments about a car that had nothing going for it but the price. How I wished we could afford a Dodge mini-van!

We kept reminding each other that God blessed us with $2,750 to purchase the car we needed, not the car we wanted. But there really wasn't much to look at.

Just when we were about to give up and go home, I suggested we shop at one more used car lot. There we saw a beautiful Oldsmobile Bravado—the best car we'd seen all day. And I admit we started to drool over it. Maybe we could go for it. Frank remarked, "Wouldn't this be nice? We could take out a loan and go into debt."

But Frank regained his senses when the dealer came and asked how much we wanted to spend—or at least he nearly regained his senses. Frank said, "Oh, $3000."

The dealer didn't laugh. He just said, "What type of car are you looking for?"

"A Dodge mini-van," Frank answered.

"I'll go check with the manager. Maybe he took in something today and hasn't sent it to the wholesaler yet."

He returned in a few minutes. "As a matter of fact, we have one used Dodge mini-van that was traded today, and my manager will take $3000."

By now my husband was saying to himself, "The Lord gave us $2,750—not $3,000—so why did I say that?" Though we probably could have managed the difference without going into debt, we didn't really want to.

The salesman pointed out a clean, great-looking Dodge mini-van—a winner compared to the ones we had driven earlier. We told the dealer we needed time to pray. After we prayed, we felt all right about purchasing it, but my husband was still kicking himself for saying $3000.

By now it was the end of the day. Frank told the dealer we would take the mini-van if they would check for any major problems. The manager said okay, but . . . if they inspected it and found something wrong, they would be obligated to fix it; in which case the price of the car could go up. Having explained that, the dealer slid a piece of paper over to us: $2,750 final price. Take it or leave it.

We could hardly believe our eyes. Without even discussing it with him, we had gotten a good car—and it was a good car—for the exact price we could afford.

Apparently, God is even in the used car business. How easy it would have been for us to give in to our desire for the more expensive car and go into debt. But we were blessed by waiting for the car of God's choice, one we could pay for.

Sandra and Frank saw God meet both their needs and their wants—miraculously and on the very day they asked.

HER FOOD SUPPLY KEPT MULTIPLYING

Jackie Womack knows what it is like to have God multiply her food supply. How he does it, she doesn't know. But she remembers a particular week some ten years ago when he answered her prayer with a miracle.

Jackie was home caring for five small children while her salesman husband was away trying to make some money for the family.

Their food supply was scarce. All she had was one loaf of bread, one gallon of milk, a carton of eggs, a box of cereal, and a little bit of hamburger meat.

Every time she cooked a meal, miraculously there seemed to be just enough left for the next meal. And so it went the rest of the week.

But one night the supply dried up. She served dinner, and then her cupboard was bare. She and the children prayed together, thanking God for his coming provision. She was careful not to let the children know the food had finally run out.

After she got the children into bed, Jackie sat down to read her Bible. She paused from her reading and prayed, "Lord, it says here in Psalms that your children will never beg for bread. I am going to believe that you will somehow provide food for our table. I believe we will never have to beg for food. Thank you. ...."

Before she even finished praying, the phone rang. The friend on the other end said, "As I was praying tonight, I became concerned for your family. I felt I should call and tell you that tomorrow I am giving you $150 for your needs. I couldn't go to bed until I told you what God impressed on my heart."

Not only had Jackie seen the multiplication of the food during the week, but in answer to the prayers of her children and herself, God spoke to someone to provide money to stock her pantry.

Jackie was amazed at the intricate timing of the Lord. Within minutes of the children's prayers, and precisely as she was calling upon the Lord to fulfill his promise, God answered specifically through someone who heard and obeyed the leading of the Spirit. Jackie was overwhelmed by God's goodness and spent the next moments praising and thanking him. In fact, this experience became a marker in Jackie's life, one experience among many that she often looks back upon—reminders of God's faithfulness, reminders that he is a sure and stable foundation on which she and her children can be secure.

GIVE IN OBEDIENCE

When chiropractor Perry Hefty's accountant called him on April 1, it wasn't an April Fool's joke. "Sit down, Perry. I have some shocking news. We underestimated your taxes. You owe $10,000."

Income tax filing was just two weeks away. Perry and his wife, Arlys, had only $1000 set aside for taxes. Where would the additional money come from? They had no idea. But they prayed God would supply.

A few days later while praying about a missionary friend named Carolyn, Perry felt God wanted him to give her their $1000. Shaking his head in bewilderment, Perry continued his prayer: "Lord, if that is you, tell my wife too. Then let her tell me."

Later that day Arlys called. "I think we are to give Carolyn $1000." Perry could hardly believe what he was hearing. But they acted in faith and wrote a check.

"We didn't give to get, as we've heard some people do. We just gave to our missionary friend because we considered it obedience to what God wanted us to do." Perry told me. "And we kept praying about our own need, trusting God to meet it, though we had no idea how."

Perry went to an out-of-state conference he had already committed to attend. While he was there Arlys phoned him. "Sit down," she said.

"I don't want to sit down again," he responded, fearing more financial bad news.

"It's good news," said Arlys, who worked part time in his office. "We have all the money we need for the income tax! Some of our older accounts, past due for months, were suddenly paid; and of course, you know we've picked up some new accounts in the past few days. We have all we need—and it's not even April 15."

After Perry came home, the Heftys learned the $1000 donation they had made had saved Carolyn's mission from closing its doors. "Very timely and an example of how important it is to be obedient in our giving," Perry said.

As our Lord said, "Give, and it will be given to you. A good measure, pressed down, shaken together and running over, will be poured into your lap. For with the measure you use, it will be measured to you" (Luke 6:38).

A FISHY PROVISION

Financial provisions don't always come in the form of money. Take the way God chose to feed a group of mission workers.

A skeleton crew of volunteers busied themselves repairing an old ship docked in a Grecian port. This was no small ship, 522 feet long—almost the length of two football fields—and weighing twelve thousand tons. Built in

Italy in 1953 for long ocean voyages, she could hold more than six hundred people.

The scraping, painting, repairing, and renovations were for a good purpose: to convert the ship into a sailing hospital that would provide medical aid to the poor in underprivileged nations. Workers would also share the Gospel. As a "mercy ship" she was renamed *Anastasis,* which is a Greek word meaning "Resurrection."

The *Anastasis* had belonged to the Youth With A Mission organization for more than three years, and it still was not ready to sail. Finances were in short supply, as were ship helpers.

In October 1981, Don Stephens, director of the Mercy Ship project, encouraged the crew and their families to fast throughout forty days, the amount of time Jesus had fasted at the beginning of his ministry. People could sign up to fast for a meal or a day—so that as a group they "covered" every day with prayer, asking God for direction about the ministry's future. And each morning before starting the day's work, everyone met for prayer. They asked God for money to complete the ship's repairs so they could finally embark on their ministry.

One morning as they neared the end of the forty-day fast, they gathered for prayer at their usual location, in a sea-view room of the rented hotel where they lived, halfway between Athens and Corinth. Suddenly their attention was distracted by a host of fish jumping out of the water onto the beach. They rushed outside to get a better view. About 150 yards in front of the hotel, fish were throwing themselves out of the water. Some leaped into the air and landed at the feet of a few Mercy Ship team members, who started scooping them up as fast as they could. The children were dismissed from their classes to join in the catch.

Dr. Christine Aroney-Sine, who was on the scene that day, writes about this amazing event:

We marshalled our resources, assembling wheelbarrows, buckets, plastic bags and any other receptacles we could find. Chattering excitedly, we all scurried around the beach, peering into pools and behind rocks, to capture the miraculous harvest. We dragged our catch toward the kitchen and began counting. How incredible it was. Over 8000 fish stranded themselves on the beach that day. The local people came and stared in amazement—they had never seen anything like it before.

We prayed and rejoiced and sang, marvelling at the incredible way God answered our prayers for direction. None of us ever expected anything this spectacular or unusual. What an incredible indication that God was still with us. It seemed symbolic of a promise of things to come, a promise of the abundant harvest we would one day see from the *Anastasis*. We felt God was assuring us of his blessing on our ministry and it gave us new hope for the future.

Amazingly, our chief cook happened to be a Norwegian. That seemed like a miracle too. He knew exactly how to prepare and preserve those fish and soon had us all working hard cleaning our catch.

Much to my disgust, as I discovered over the next few days, miracles often have a negative side as well as a positive one, and require quite a bit of effort on our part to accomplish. It takes a long time and a lot of people to gut and clean over 8000 fish. Everyone played a part.

We pulled the dining tables together and set up a rather smelly production line. It was hard to maintain our enthusiasm as we gutted, salted and preserved our harvest. Soon we all reeked with the smell and our hands ached from using inadequate implements. . . .

As we processed the fish I learned a very important lesson. I realized, with horror, how easily our rejoicing could turn to grumbling. It made me think of the children of Israel in the desert. All of us have the potential to be like them, I surmised, and God's provision, if not handled with gratitude can look like a curse. It took days to adequately clean our catch and they formed a supplement to our diet for many months to come. By the time they were finished some of the crew were heartily sick of our "miracle fish." It was hard to remember the excitement of the miracle and God's abundant generosity in a slim season.[2]

Finally the ship was ready to sail—through the Mediterranean Sea and across the Atlantic toward the Panama Canal, the Pacific Ocean, and finally Los Angeles. During a five-month stay in California, hospital equipment was installed and cargo for refugee relief was stored in the ship's hold, generously provided by American Christians.

The *Anastasis* has been sailing ever since, carrying out its mission of healing and evangelism. The "fish miracle" of the early *Anastasis* crew is told and retold to those who join the ship—an example of God's provision and care for their mission.

PROTECTED FILES

Our businesses are important to us, as they provide the things we need for our daily lives. Things can also happen there that need prayer for God to be our Provider, as Toni Weaver testifies in this story.

At 3:00 A.M. on November 4, 1994, the shrill ring of the telephone jarred us awake. My husband, Dewayne, answered it. Someone from our alarm service was calling to say the alarm at our roofing company was going off and they had notified the police. Our office was about eleven miles away. My husband hurried to see what had triggered the alarm.

Middle of the night phone calls unsettle me. I began to pray. I could imagine burglary and vandalism and wondered what Dewayne might encounter when he arrived at our business. Fifteen minutes later he called. "You need to come right away," he said. "The building is on fire."

I rushed to get dressed. As I drove to the office, I prayed all the way. Mainly, I asked God to let angels protect the records in my file cabinets. All our corporate records were in them. Not only did I have our customers' records, but I had a payroll of fifty men. If those files were destroyed, it would takes days, or even months, to redo them.

When I arrived, our modular office was engulfed in flames. Fire trucks and firefighters were everywhere. They had broken out the doors and windows. Smoke enclosed the area. What I could see of the inside of the office was black and wet.

The firefighters began hauling charred furniture outside. Finally, they dragged my file cabinets outside. They were black and scorched, but the files inside were saved! I wanted to shout Hallelujah so loud everyone around could hear. Instead, I silently thanked God for this miracle answer to prayer. My files were the only thing salvageable from the fire.

Because my computer had been destroyed, I did lose data and had to rebuild the employee files. But I had a starting place because of the files that were saved.

The night of the fire, the Lord impressed on me that he would turn this tragedy into a praise report. I did not know how, but I was convinced he would do so. I trusted his provision.

We discovered after the fire that our office building was underinsured by $24,000, as we carried only coverage for the "hard cost" of the office. What a blow! Nevertheless, we invested some extra money, and by January we started the construction of a new concrete office. On April 1 it was completed—beautiful, permanent, and larger and better than the previous one.

When we received our property tax bill, the new building had been appraised for $29,000 more than it had actually cost us to build. This was God's way of redeeming our loss. We had been able to rebuild for much less than the market rate, thus increasing our value. Someday, when we sell the building, we will realize the gain.

I looked up the word "restoration" in the dictionary and found that it means "to restore to an improved position." This is precisely what God did. He is a God of restoration, of rebuilding. He gave us an even better building; he turned a tragedy into a victory.

Sometimes when we do lose material things, it is difficult to see beyond the loss. But Toni and Dewayne today have a thriving business in a much better office building. The most important lesson to learn, however, is that we must trust in God to provide for our needs and must place ourselves in his wise and loving care.

THE CHRISTMAS GIFT

This final story is my own, one that I frequently use to remind myself of our Lord's care and provision.

The Sunday before Christmas 1979, I slumped into a church pew, waiting for the service to begin. I couldn't choke back the tears. It was our last Christmas with good friends, our last in Titusville, Florida, the community where our children had grown up. Two weeks earlier my husband had decided to take early retirement. We were going to move to the piney woods of northwest Florida, near Destin, where we had a plot of land.

Yes, I had agreed to his retiring, because he believed God was directing him to do this now. But I worried and fretted over finances. We had two children still in college and one in high school, with almost no savings for tuition. His retirement pay was barely enough to support the two of us, let alone keep kids in college. And his finding a good-paying job would be difficult, considering his age, his physical condition (back problems had kept him in traction for three months), and the rural area to which we were going.

Hunched over in the pew, I was anxious and trying to muster up some faith. On one hand I was doubting that God would meet our family needs; on the other I was berating myself for not trusting him. Finally, I asked God to give me assurance that he would meet our needs. Little did I expect him to use Helen, a fiery little widow with a tightly curled auburn chignon, to speak to my heart.

Each year just before Christmas, the church took up a special offering to help send doctors, missionaries, and technicians around the world. That Sunday, just as families were to bring their offerings to the altar, the pastor asked Helen to come to the podium and relate a story she had told him earlier in the week.

"Most of you know I've been a widow five years and live on a very limited income," she said. "When I prayed about how much I was to contribute to our Christmas mission offering, two hundred dollars kept coming to my mind. I had no any idea how I could give that kind of money. But I wrote the amount down. I frequently prayed about my offering, thanking the Lord that he would provide this amount.

"After Thanksgiving, I held to a promise I had made to my daughter—to search the attic of our old homeplace for some legal papers she needed. While rummaging around up there, I spied a small tin labeled 'electrical tape.' Thinking that could be of use to me, I slipped the container into my pocket, climbed out of the attic, and went about my other chores. Imagine my surprise later when I opened the can to use the tape. Inside I found a tight roll of bills—exactly two hundred dollars."

Helen excitedly waved the small round can in the air. "In here is God's mission money—for his kids in need," she exclaimed.

I wondered how many years earlier Helen's husband had hid that money away for a rainy day—never realizing it would be discovered at the exact moment it was needed to meet a prayer request.

Helen's story had struck me to the heart. Drying my tears, I straightened my shoulders and smiled. Surely my heavenly Father had more than a tin of money tucked away to help meet our needs!

Over the next few months, as I prayed for ways to meet our living expenses, I would remember Helen and her tin can and thank God in advance that money was forthcoming.

And God supplied our needs. Our children found summer jobs to help with college tuition. I started writing for magazines. A garden kept our refrigerator full. In time my husband landed a job he could handle with his physical limitations. Our oldest child graduated. Our youngest started college. And so it went.

Did I doubt God? I admit there were still times when my faith for finances faltered. But then I would think of Helen and affirm God's faithfulness with a prayer of thanksgiving.[3]

As I look back, I see God's hand in that move, which allowed us to be near my Mom as she fought a battle against cancer. God's intervention and his provision are hard not to acknowledge. He knew what was ahead of us when we didn't and he always made a way.

This story often reminds me that we serve a God whom the Hebrews called Jehovah-Jireh, God Our Provider (see Genesis 22:1–14).

And our Provider is a God who knows how to work miracles.

Praying the Scriptures

THE GRACIOUS GIVER

"For I know the plans I have for you," declares the LORD, "plans to prosper you and not to harm you, plans to give you hope and a future."

JEREMIAH 29:11

Which of you, if his son asks for bread, will give him a stone? Or if he asks for a fish, will give him a snake? If you, then, though you are evil, know how to give good gifts to your children, how much more will your Father in heaven give good gifts to those who ask him!

MATTHEW 7:9–11

Give, and it will be given to you. A good measure, pressed down, shaken together and running over, will be poured into your lap. For with the measure you use, it will be measured to you.

LUKE 6:38

The King will reply, "I tell you the truth, whatever you did for one of the least of these brothers of mine, you did for me."

MATTHEW 25:40

Honor the LORD with your wealth, with the firstfruits of all your crops; then your barns will be filled to over-flowing. . . .

PROVERBS 3:9–10A

Know that the LORD is God. It is he who has made us, and we are his; we are his people, the sheep of his pasture. . . . For the LORD is good and his love endures forever.

PSALM 100:3–5A

PART THREE

Miracles of the Heart

All a man's ways seem right to him, but the LORD *weighs the heart.*

PROVERBS 21:2

At the heart of your need is waiting a gentle understanding Savior.

ANONYMOUS

*T*he greatest miracles often happen at the spiritual center of our lives, where our fear, mistrust, selfishness, anger, and bitterness are transformed by the power of the Holy Spirit.

We long to have loving relationships at home, at church, and at work. Yet so many times we feel at odds with those we are supposed to love the most—our impossible, alcoholic parents, our rebelling children, or our irritating spouses. Can anything change us? Can anything change them?

Sometimes it seems easier to believe that God can provide for us financially than to believe he will transform people or relationships, or to believe God can save us in a car accident than to trust him to free us from long-standing addictions such as eating disorders. It seems easier to trust God for an exterior change than for an interior change—in us or others.

One of the most dramatic heart changes recorded in the Bible occurred in a man named Saul, who by his own admission "was once a blasphemer and a persecutor and a violent man . . . [acting] in ignorance and unbelief" (1 Timothy 1:13). On his way to Damascus to wipe out Christians, he was suddenly blinded by a bright light and struck to the ground. Jesus spoke from heaven, "Saul, Saul, why do you persecute me?" (Acts 9:4).

Three days later as a man named Ananias prayed for him; Saul was filled with the Holy Spirit, regained his sight, was baptized, and immediately started preaching that Jesus was the Son of God. Using the name of Paul, he became one of the most powerful early Christian missionaries. A large portion of our New Testament comes from his writings.

Many miracles of the heart are less dramatic than Paul's Damascus Road conversion. And some miracles that bring us into spiritual or emotional freedom take place long after we have initially placed our trust in Christ.

As you look to Christ for a heart miracle, consider your heart motive. Do I want my husband changed because I want it to be easier for me when he comes home? Or do I really want him to be the man God intended him to be? Do I want my child brought into a right relationship because she is a constant embarrassment to me among my friends? Or do I sincerely want her to fulfill God's purpose for her life? Do I want my own heart cleansed?

As you pray, be honest with God, but also give him permission to purify your motives. Allow him to make you a partner in his work—a prayer partner. Ours is not a passive role. We may never sit back and say, "It's up to you, God." No, he invites us to be persistent in our prayers. Ultimately, as we pray, we begin to desire the will of God, and we will not stop until we, in faith, with our focus on him, "pray through"—feel a release. God wants to peel back our own heart's crust—the hard coating we have allowed to build up over the years—not only to make us whole, but also to use us as his miracle instrument of healing to others.

The following stories of how God intervenes will help you remember to turn to God whether you are facing a small problem or one that threatens to overwhelm you. Remember, there is not anything—no relationship or situation or heart sickness—that cannot be changed by the power of our awesome God.

Many of us start praying for a miracle when we have exhausted every other remedy. And while it would be better if we were to begin rather than end with prayer, God hears our cries, no matter how dark the situation facing us may seem.

THE WORD OF GOD HEALS HER SICK HEART

Frances Jackson tells of the night she thought she was going to die. As a doctor's daughter, she was familiar enough with warning signals to know she was in serious danger. Little did she know God's Word would be the prescription she needed. This story involves the healing of a physical heart. But what Frances learned about prayer can apply to any desire for spiritual heart healing. Frances, now seventy-two-years old and still enjoying an active life, describes her dilemma.

Suddenly, in the middle of the night, a blow like a sledge hammer hit my chest. My heart "flopped" and then pounded violently. Struggling between gulps, I woke my husband. "I'm having a heart attack, Dan. Call 911."

After a week of intensive tests and examinations by a team of specialists at Bay Front Hospital, I learned that my heart's mitral valve had suffered extensive damage. My chances for a full recovery were questionable.

Doctors sent me home, but even there no amount of rest or sleep helped. The slightest exertion caused my heart to jump out of rhythm—skipping, flopping, pounding; then a strange stillness would come over me as though my heart had stopped altogether.

Within six months I had lost thirty pounds. I was short of breath and frail. Medications brought on side effects that nearly killed me. Anxiety and fear mounted. Often I would sit with my hand on the phone, wondering if I should call 911—afraid I might die before I could dial the numbers. My life had become a nightmare, a living hell.

A second heart specialist offered the hope of open heart surgery, replacing a valve. But even those supposedly encouraging words struck terror to the depths of my spirit; I knew I could not survive such a procedure. Hoping for some other course of treatment, I wrote to a doctor friend at Duke Medical Center in North Carolina, explaining my plight.

Meanwhile my sister Betty arrived from out of town, announcing, "God is going to heal you. It isn't too late!"

Betty played a cassette tape about healing. The speaker's gentle voice assured me Jesus could heal me. The speaker told her own story; Jesus had healed her enlarged heart, and she had medical records to prove the healing.

I absorbed every word. She encouraged her listeners to meditate for three days on everything Jesus said about healing. She read the Scripture passages aloud on the tape, and I followed word by word in my Bible. Then she said, "Pray out loud. Talk to God. Tell him your needs and ask for his help."

I prayed aloud, "Heavenly Father, my heart is sick and broken. It looks as though my time to die has arrived. I need air to breathe. I feel ill. I am frightened. My strength is drifting away. I know I can't hold on much longer. I don't want to die. But if I must, I want to go to heaven. Forgive my sins. Help me, Lord, please help me."

I wept profusely. In total surrender I released my life and my body to God. As I "let go," I envisioned death in a black robe walking away from me. A gentle warmness flowed through me, a glorious refreshing freedom. Relief came—as though a ten-ton truck had been lifted off me.

"I feel strong. I feel healed!" I shouted in amazement. My weakness had become strength. Illness had become wellness. Pain was exchanged for joy; anxiety for peace; fear for faith. I thought, *This must be what God means when he gives blessings of abundant life to his children.*

I opened the front door. The grass looked greener and the sky bluer; the sun shone with more sparkle. "Thank you, Lord, for bringing me out of darkness into God's marvelous light," I prayed.

I headed for the mailbox, which contained a letter from Dr. McPherson at Duke University, urging me to come at once. I knew God had healed me, yet I wanted to go to Duke for clinical confirmation that would seal this miracle.

I decided to tell no one about my healing except my husband and my sister. Two days later I boarded a plane, heading for Duke and carrying all my medical records. Once there I was connected to a heart monitor for ten days. I underwent every conceivable examination. On the tenth day, a smiling Dr. McPherson stood by my bed. "Well, I don't know what to say except that your heart and general health seem fine—perfectly normal in every way. I can't say I understand why this is so, because your previous medical records indicate quite the opposite. And valves don't heal; valves are replaced."

This was the confirmation I had been praying for. "God healed me!" I explained. "I was afraid to tell you for fear I'd be sent to the psychiatric ward." We both laughed.

"Let's just thank God for your miracle and give him full credit," he said, shaking hands one last time.

I suffered my heart attack in May 1980. My miracle healing was six months later. I have been in excellent health without being sick a day for fifteen years. God has truly healed my heart.

Frances discovered the power of the Word of God as she meditated on healing Scriptures—just the prescription she needed for her physical and spiritual heart healing. May it bring encouragement to you if you are waiting in faith for your own needed breakthrough.

A NEW HEART AND A RENEWED MARRIAGE

This story starts in Colorado nearly twenty-three years ago, when Carolyn Sundseth asked her husband, Vic, for a separation; their marriage had been plagued with his drinking, and she had had it. Just before Vic moved away—far away to Kona, Hawaii, to be near his son Gale—Vic had a spiritual encounter with God. But Carolyn was skeptical of his God talk. She couldn't believe he would really change, so she went ahead with the divorce.

But in November 1974, at their sons' insistence, she agreed to see Vic while on a vacation in Hawaii. Immediately she could tell he was changed. He asked her forgiveness for the ways he had let her down for so many years. He was a new man, and Carolyn noticed. When she went with Vic to visit some of his friends, she let them pray for God to transform her life.

A month later, Christmas Day 1974, Vic had a heart attack while driving home from spending the morning with his son. He got himself to his room and immediately prayed. "God, if it's my time to go, it's all right with me. But I have so many things left I'd like to do. Lord, will you give me a new heart?" Suffering from congenital heart irregularities, Vic knew a new heart was what he really needed.

Because he had no insurance, Vic didn't immediately go to a doctor. He made himself as comfortable as he could and kept praying. That evening several friends rallied around him, anointing him with oil and praying for his healing. One man unknowingly repeated the exact same prayer Vic had prayed earlier, asking God to give Vic a new heart.

When Carolyn heard of Vic's heart attack—which was confirmed by a doctor—she wrote him. Would he like to come back to Colorado to recuperate? She would let him stay in their sons' empty bedroom while he regained his health. She would even buy him round trip plane tickets if his doctors approved his flying.

Vic agreed and returned "home" to recuperate. While there he went to their family doctor, who ran tests and compared them to his old file records. Finally, he called them in to talk.

"Look here," he said, pointing to Vic's EKG, "This heart has no infarction [tissue damage that usually results from a heart attack]. This is like a brand new heart. I do not believe in miracles, so I cannot explain it, but this is not Vic's heart. This is a new, totally healthy heart, the heart of a thirty-year-old athlete."

A new heart! That's what Vic and the others back in Hawaii had prayed for him. And that's what the doctor claimed to see.

And as for Carolyn, she found herself falling in love with Vic—a new man in spirit—all over again. She says, "God, who performed a complete heart transplant for Vic, kept him in Denver for another miracle, as he miraculously restored our love." They were secretly remarried on February 15, 1975—their twenty-third wedding anniversary. Today, eighty-three-year-old Vic enjoys playing golf in Van, Texas; they live near Mercy Ships headquarters, where Carolyn has been a long time ambassador, recruiting for missions.

Through the mercy of God Vic had received the heart of a young, healthy man. What's more, both he and Carolyn had turned their spiritual hearts toward God, who brought them to each other—a miracle of reconciliation!

BLESS, DON'T CURSE

Ferrah Stuck and her husband were amazed at God's work in their neighborhood. Even though the story took years to unfold, its resolution became evident to the Stucks in what they call "one of God's miraculous suddenlies." Ferrah tells her story:

Seventeen years ago when we moved into our home, we asked if our neighbors would be interested in sharing the expense of a backyard fence. They said yes; but when the fence was up and my husband went to collect, the husband refused, arguing that the ugly side of the fence faced him. Why should he have to pay?

Eventually I started praying for all my neighbors. Some days I'd walk our neighborhood, praying blessings for each family. Two years ago at Christmastime, I invited women in my neighborhood to come to a Christmas party. Only seven came, but my backyard neighbor was one of them.

A year and a half later the woman knocked on my door. She held out an open hand containing two $100 bills and one $50 bill—$250 total. I stared at it, puzzled, and then she reached out and put the bills into my hand.

She said, "We have owed you this amount since not paying you for our part of the backyard fence seventeen years ago. It has been on my heart to make it right."

I invited her in, but she had to hurry home to put away groceries. As I thanked her, I gave her a hug. Then I went into my bedroom, knelt beside my bed, and asked God to forgive me for any bitterness I had felt toward her. I prayed a blessing over her and her family.

When I showed my husband the unexpected gift—the old debt finally paid—we discussed many ways we could spend it. Because the money was something we had released to the Lord years ago, we decided to give it to the Aglow women's ministry, which was purchasing "A House of Prayer For All Nations" near Seattle. Hundreds will pray in that house for people around the world, just as I have prayed for my neighborhood.

In teaching the Beatitudes, Jesus said to give to the one who asks you, to love your enemies, and to pray for those who persecute you (see Matthew 5:42–44). As Ferrah and her husband lived out this Scripture, they saw visible evidence of God's work, warming the hearts of their neighbors.

A DIVINE APPOINTMENT

I believe God brings certain people into our lives at specific times—by his divine appointment. My husband, LeRoy, had a divine appointment while hospitalized and in traction for back problems.

Each day the nurse told him he would be getting a roommate named Eugene Matthews. But the new roommate didn't come. On the third day, he finally walked in, wearing street clothes. He had been in the intensive care unit having tests because of his heart condition. The nurses had told him to go to LeRoy's room and wait for further orders. He chose a highback chair near the foot of LeRoy's bed and began to talk.

He poured out his life story in graphic detail, explaining his rough life as a pipe fitter and welder. He had moved from place to place as jobs opened up and admitted he had done a lot of "carousing, drinking, and cursing" with the worst of the men. His first marriage ended in divorce. He hadn't had contact with his son in years.

Sure, he used to go to church, he said. But he hadn't been inside a church in forty years. Churchgoers were a bunch of hypocrites! Before long, however, he was asking LeRoy a lot of life and death questions. His heart condition had obviously caused him to question his own future. Did he have long to live? Had his life counted for anything?

LeRoy took him on a journey from the beginning to the end of the Bible, just talking. Mostly he emphasized Jesus' coming to earth and dying for those who would accept his forgiveness. He kept saying that Jesus provides a place with him in heaven for those who acknowledge him as Savior.

"What church do you go to?" Eugene interrupted LeRoy.

"It doesn't matter what church I go to. What matters is that you know Jesus. He helps us live our lives in a way that pleases him."

"Wait, tell me what church you go to!"

LeRoy finally told him.

After three hours of discussion, a nurse came in, "Mr. Matthews, the doctor has decided to discharge you. Why don't you call someone to take you home now?"

LeRoy shook hands with Eugene and said a short prayer asking God's blessings over him.

Three weeks later, on a Sunday night, LeRoy was home and able to go to church. The pastor made the following announcement, "If you were recently in the hospital with a man named Eugene Matthews, would you contact our church office? We received a letter this week requesting that his church membership be transferred to our congregation. But his wife called to say he died last night. She wants to contact the man who met him in the hospital."

We phoned the woman, and she told us an incredible story. That Saturday night, while holding her hand as they watched television, Eugene had quietly died. In the three weeks since he had been in the hospital, her husband had been a transformed man.

He had asked her forgiveness for years of verbal abuse. He had phoned his sister and asked her forgiveness. He had been in touch with his son from whom he'd long been estranged. He had quit yelling at the neighborhood children. Finally, every night he had asked his wife to read the Bible aloud to him.

She asked LeRoy, "Will you have a graveside service for him? We don't know a preacher. Eugene didn't have any friends, but maybe a few family members will come. I used to go to church myself before we moved here, but I stopped because he resented it so much. But I prayed for him every night. It was wonderful living with a changed man for the past three weeks. He told me you were the one who made him start thinking about how he needed to change."

I drove LeRoy to the cemetery for the graveside service. Briefly he shared what he had told Eugene in the hospital. We shook hands with the ten people who came, including his son. One neighbor said she used to pray for him because he cursed at her kids when they got near his fence. Remarkably, she said, he had recently laughed with and talked to her children.

We have visited his widow several times since her husband's death. "He found such peace just before he died. It was beautiful to watch the change in him," she said.

A divine appointment? Yes. Who ever heard of a hospital roommate who didn't stay long enough to pull back the sheets of the bed? Why hadn't the nurse told him to wait in the hall? In God's plan he chose not to heal Eugene's physical heart, but what a dramatic miracle he worked in his spirit and home—in answer to the prayers of people wishing his stony heart would soften.

When we wholeheartedly yield to God, he takes our heart of stone and in return gives us a heart of flesh. He puts a new spirit within us. You might say that we get a heart transplant (see Ezekiel 11:19).

AN ACCIDENT CHANGED MY HEART

Hilda Forehand had to undergo multiple surgeries. But in the process, God's surgery removed crust from her heart—a hardness she didn't even know was there. She tells her own story:[1]

We were just winding up a wonderful vacation on Phillips Inlet in northwest Florida. We had spent the afternoon fishing and were on our way in for a late supper. "Honey, this will be my last chance. Please let me ski the rest of the way in," I called to my husband, Hilliard, over the roar of the boat motor.

"Okay, one last time," he said. At forty years old, wearing my new red bikini, I felt as young as our teenagers. Hilliard stopped the boat and threw the skis out into the water, and I dove in. I slipped on the skis and waited. He always circled the boat around to bring the rope near for me to grab. But this time something went wrong; the boat's steering cable jammed, making it impossible to turn.

I watched helplessly as the boat headed straight for me. In a split second the propeller sliced into my face and right arm like a butcher's cleaver carving prime rib.

The next thing I was aware of was someone in white cutting my throat to perform a tracheotomy. I felt no pain, only numbness. But I distinctly heard one doctor say, "Every bone in her face is broken. Her brain has got to be damaged. From all that force hitting her there's just no way her brain could have escaped."

I wanted to shout, "No, it isn't." But I couldn't talk.

Yes, every bone in my face was broken. My eye sockets were crushed, leaving my eyes without support. A portion of my upper lip was cut away. My chin bone was split in half. My mouth was almost entirely gutted except for my tongue.

For three days I lay in intensive care in that hospital in Panama City, Florida. My condition was too critical for surgery. No visitors were allowed, but more than a hundred people traveled from my small hometown of Enterprise, Alabama, just to ask about me. Prayer vigils were set up in several states. I lay like a corpse; yet everything in me fought to survive.

I was airlifted to a hospital in Birmingham. When I drifted out of my coma, I felt unbearable pain. Finally, five days after I arrived, I was wheeled into the operating room for thirteen hours of surgery.

Seven more times in the next two months I went back under the surgeon's knife. I was plagued by pain and more pain. The doctors used my bone fragments and plastic plates to reconstruct cheekbones; they inserted plastic eye sockets to hold my eyes, placed a splint in the top of my mouth, and implanted seventeen teeth into my gums. In the final surgery, they bored holes in my forehead and inserted wires to hold my face in place. Staring in the mirror, I was horrified at the sight: a woman with metal wires like antennae sticking in the air. My face was distorted beyond recognition. "My career as an interior decorator is ruined," I wept.

When I was released to go home for a while, my daughter patiently squirted liquids through a syringe into my mouth. One day when I complained, she told me to be thankful for soup; it was keeping me alive.

All of a sudden I saw how ungrateful I had been. Over the next four months I had plenty of time to think about my life and realize my priorities had been wrong. My days had been full of activity, but empty of meaning. I thought a lot, too, about God, but I didn't know how to contact him.

Finally, I was on my way back to Birmingham to get the wires removed. That procedure went as planned, but doctors determined that my appendix was on the verge of rupturing. More surgery, and then my intestines quit functioning. Tubes were put back down my nose. IVs were started in both arms. This pain was worse than any I had experienced before. As waves of nausea rolled over me, I begged God to let me die.

Hilliard left the room and returned with a big green book. "This is the new Living Bible, and I'm going to start reading it to you," he announced.

"Why?" I wondered. We had Bibles we took to church. Why sit and read to me from a version I had never heard of?

But Hilliard read on for hours. Some passages comforted me—especially Jesus' words, "There are many homes up there where my Father lives, and I am going to prepare them for your coming. . . . I am the Way—yes, and the Truth and the Life. No one can get to the Father except by means of me . . ." (John 14: 2, 6 LB). Suddenly I saw it: Jesus was my way to God, the only way. He had prepared a place in heaven for me. While the words offered comfort, they did not ease my excruciating pain.

By Sunday morning, I was still pleading silently with God to take me to heaven, and I let my secret desire "slip." Hilliard hadn't left me in days, but now he needed to go out for shaving supplies. "Be good to the children when I'm gone," I whispered as he walked toward the door.

He pivoted around, with hurt etched in his deep blue eyes. "You can't give up now, Hilda. You've come through too much. Mrs. Cross, a lady down the hall, isn't expected to live. But you are. You are going to live."

Just as I asked God one more time to take me on "home," Mrs. Evans, a nurse came in and bathed me. She was humming a song I remembered from childhood: "God Will Take Care of You"—"through every day."

As she hummed, the room filled with light that seemed to penetrate through me. I could feel the presence of Jesus. He was so real, so personal—there, with me. "Oh, dear God," I managed to whisper as I watched light dance through prisms, creating rainbows around me. I had a sudden inner drive to live, to see each one in my family know the Lord and his presence just as I was experiencing him at that moment.

Awed by what was happening, I prayed again but changed my plea. "Lord, if you let me live, I will spend the rest of my life living for you." There was no bargaining, no more begging him to remove pain, no more wishing to die.

Over the next few hours my pain and nausea left. I started joking with the nurse. The tube placed in my abdomen to pump out poisons was removed the next morning. The IVs were soon gone too, and nurses' aides began walking me up and down the hall.

Two days later I had an urge to go pray for the woman down the hall, Mrs. Cross. Hilliard had said she was dying; her fever was so high she was packed in ice. But I had never prayed aloud for anyone. What would she think? For six hours I fought an inward voice that whispered, "Go pray for her."

Finally, I threw the covers back and inched myself out of bed. Clinging to the sides of the walls, I shuffled slowly down to her room. A sign on the door read: "Family Only," but that didn't stop me. Pushing the door open, I tiptoed over to her bed and laid my hand on her knee. She opened her eyes.

"I'm praying for you," I explained.

"Oh, thank you," she whispered.

"Lord Jesus, I don't know how to pray for this lady. But will you please heal her?" I didn't know how else to pray because I had never heard anyone pray for a miracle before.

The next morning when the nurse came to take my vital signs, she was obviously excited. "Mrs. Cross's doctors are amazed at her rapid recovery. She's going to be fine." I uttered a silent prayer of thanks.

Mrs. Cross went home two days later. She may have had a miracle. But I definitely did as well! I went home with wires removed from my face and with the crust removed from my heart. I was now more sensitive to other people's needs and less focused on my own.

It has been twenty-five years since my boating accident. My face will never be whole—not in this life. But I am glad to be alive! Through my sufferings, I discovered a personal Lord who cares about me. He has straightened out my priorities. I am no longer too busy for God, my husband, my children, or neighbors. Moreover, my own metamorphosis prompted a change in my husband and four children. They have all turned their hearts toward him.

MY SONG CHANGED THROUGH FORGIVENESS

This next story is about my own heart and the alteration God wanted done in me. It is amazing how you can be in church most of your life and still allow your past to keep you in bondage.

Hate him. Hate him. Hate him. Hate him. All night long the wheels of the train echoed the dreary song in my heart, as I sobbed myself to sleep in the berth below my mother and six-year-old sister. *Hate him. Hate him. Hate him.*

All I could think about was lashing out to hurt the one who was hurting me—my daddy. Poisonous thoughts shot in quick succession through my mind, like invisible darts.

How dare he do this to us? What kind of father would ship his own family away on a train?

Daddy was sending us to my aunt's in Florida. I was only twelve at the time, too timid to tell him how much I hated him for sending us away, especially at Christmastime; for making me leave behind my two brothers, all my friends, and our comfortable brick home. Unable to express my anger and hurt, I simply "closed off" my heart to him and silently vowed, "I'll never forgive him."

The same morning he put us on the train, I overheard a whisper of the ugly word—divorce. By summer it was a fact. Daddy had married his secretary. But by now Mother had custody of my two brothers whom Daddy had initially tried to keep, so in a sense we were "family" once more.

Mother worked hard to save enough to make a down payment on an old clapboard boarding house in Tallahassee. Here she could help her four children get a college education. She put in fourteen-hour days of back-breaking labor, taking care of forty boarders and feeding more than three hundred a day in shifts in her dining room. Meals were served family style, all you could eat. My sister and I had to wait tables. Whenever I heard mother cooking in the kitchen at five in the morning, the old feelings of anger and resentment toward Daddy would return.

My only contacts with my father as I grew up were a few painful visits—strained and quick, never on holidays or important occasions, and always in a neutral place with his wife present. I fell into a familiar pattern of "stuffing" my true feelings—anger, rejection, hurt.

Mother's hair turned gray, and her legs dragged with arthritic pain. The state of Florida finally condemned her old boarding house so they could build a fine state office building on the site. Mother had to take what they offered and move once more. Resentment against my daddy rose up in me again.

Although I was a Christian, I would not take responsibility for my ugly attitude. I continued to blame Daddy for Mother's failing health from having to work so hard.

He never contributed a dime toward my college, and I worked two jobs to finish it. He never sent a card when I graduated, never wrote when I married, and never acknowledged the birth of any of my three children. And all the while he and his wife lived in fine homes, enjoying the prestige that went along with their professional careers.

One day in my late thirties, something startling happened that changed my heart. While visiting Mother, I went with her to a mid-week church service where the folks who were worshiping seemed to know God in a deeper depth than I did. When the pastor invited those who wanted prayer and further instruction about the Christian life to meet afterwards in his office, I went.

I was astonished that the first issue he dealt with was unforgiveness. We needed, he said, to ask God to forgive us for holding unforgiveness toward anyone. Instantly, I thought of Daddy. I knew Jesus had taught us to pray, "Forgive us our trespasses as we forgive those who trespass against us." But could I, after all these years of pent-up hate, really forgive my father? I hung my head, pondering the question.

I now had a choice to make. I made a choice not based on my emotions or my feelings, but based on God's Word. Haltingly, I began to pray. "Lord, I choose to forgive Daddy right now." I lifted my open palms ever so slightly as though pushing this burden right into my heavenly Father's lap. Then I added, "Lord, forgive me for all the bitterness, rage, and anger I have harbored all these years. Forgive me for hating him."

Waves of love, deep love, pulsated through me. I had never known anything like it. It filled my whole body. A Bible verse I had read sometime earlier came to mind again as a promise just for me: "He will restore the hearts of the fathers to their children, and the hearts of the children to their fathers ... " (Malachi 4:6a NASB). The pastor then prayed that Jesus would live through me and that the Holy Spirit would fill me to overflowing.

Some weeks later I wrote my dad, eager to have our relationship restored. Sometimes he answered with polite letters; other times he sent hateful ones. But I was determined to remain open to him, so I continued to write.

Almost five years passed. Then one day I got a call from Daddy. He was coming alone to visit the three of his children who still lived in Florida. He had taken the bus to my sister's, and in a couple of days I was to get him and he would stay awhile with us.

It would be the first time in my married life that Daddy had been in our home overnight. I had mixed emotions! How should I greet him? I never remembered him hugging me. Could I hug him?

As I drove the one hundred and twenty miles to my sister's home, doubts assailed me. I had forgiven him, hadn't I? Too soon I was there. There, in her backyard, our eyes met. I smiled and walked to where he stood. I draped a limp arm across his bony, stooped shoulders. Just a touch was all I could manage. Yes, I had forgiven him. My heart told me I no longer hated him, but we were still strangers. A bear hug would not have been appropriate.

"God help me," I prayed. "Help me get to know this man who is my dad."

On our screened porch the next night I drew him out in conversation; I coaxed him to talk about his childhood, to spend some time reminiscing. He laughed and leaned far back in a chair, staring at the stars. I couldn't remember hearing him laugh before. It was a good sound.

At the Space Center where my husband worked, we gawked at the unbelievable array of Space Age spin-offs on display, and Daddy shook his head in disbelief. He remembered horse and buggy days; now he faced a display of spacecraft capable of going to the moon and back.

For the next two days we caught up on life that had passed us by. The hours flew. All too soon it was time for him to leave. Before he boarded the bus, I couldn't resist the strong urge to reach out and squeeze him. I hugged him tightly for a moment, as a child clutches a treasured teddy bear.

He looked full into my watering eyes and his voice broke. "How could you love me? After all I've done. After all... ?"

I couldn't answer. I was too choked up to tell about the hate I had turned over to Jesus.

But I think he knew. After three days of being with our family, joining us for family devotions, I think he knew: I loved because I had forgiven. My heart was clear of all the debris I had surrendered to Jesus the night I chose to forgive my dad.

And I had found forgiveness from God for all my bitterness, resentment, hate, and fault finding. What a load that had been.

The bus slowly rolled down the street. As it picked up momentum, the tires seemed to echo the thoughts swirling through my mind. *Forgiven. Forgiven. Forgiven.* The song had changed.[2]

I saw my Dad several times after that, always making the effort to stop by whenever I was in the state where he and his wife lived.

He was almost eighty-four when he died, outliving my mother by a dozen years. He visited me only one other time alone; and when he did, I took him by the cemetery where we children had buried Mom.

"She forgave you long ago, Dad."

Tears sprang in his eyes. "She made a lot of sacrifices for you children. By the way, I'm glad you forgave me too," he said.

Unforgiveness not only hinders our prayers from being answered, it is the one thing that chains us to the person or situation. It keeps us in bondage. Jesus said, "Forgive, and you will be forgiven" (Luke 6:37b), and the word translated as "forgive" means *to release, set at liberty, release as unchaining someone.* We, the ones who choose to forgive, are now unchained, loosed. We have given up the desire to get even.

When we are dealing with an intractable problem in our hearts, it's a good time to realize that only God's Spirit can shape us and make us into men and women who are both healed and holy. All we have to do is invite him to do so.

Praying the Scriptures
HEAL OUR HEARTS

I am the LORD, the God of all mankind. Is anything too hard for me?

JEREMIAH 32:27

Create in me a pure heart, O God, and renew a stead-fast spirit within me.

PSALM 51:10

And I pray that Christ will be more and more at home in your hearts, living within you as you trust in him.

EPHESIANS 3:17 LB

A cheerful heart is good medicine, but a crushed spirit dries up the bones.

PROVERBS 17:22

Let us then approach the throne of grace with confidence, so that we may receive mercy and find grace to help us in our time of need.

HEBREWS 4:16

And hope does not disappoint us, because God has poured out his love into our hearts by the Holy Spirit, whom he has given us.

ROMANS 5:5

If you confess with your mouth, "Jesus is Lord," and believe in your heart that God raised him from the dead, you will be saved. For it is with your heart that you believe and are justified, and it is with your mouth that you confess and are saved.

ROMANS 10: 9–10

PART FOUR

Miracles of Lost and Found

Rejoice with me; I have found my lost sheep. . . .
Rejoice with me; I have found my lost coin. . . .
But we had to celebrate and be glad, because
this brother of yours was dead and is alive
again; he was lost and is found.

LUKE 15:6B, 9B, 32

I believe in the power of the Lord who answers
prayer.

DONALD GREY BARNHOUSE

ow many times have you lost something and found it again? Did prayer play a role in finding it? Too often we forget God is both all-knowing and all-seeing. The things hidden from us are in plain sight to God.

Our prayer may also be for a lost person—lost spiritually or lost to our relationship. Our heart's deepest desire is that the lost will be found, restored to God and/or to us.

The fifteenth chapter of Luke has been called "The Lost and Found Chapter" because it deals with three lost things, each precious to the owner: a shepherd's lost sheep, a woman's lost coin, and a father's lost son. In each case the lost is found, and each story ends with shared rejoicing. The lessons we learn from this chapter can be applied to our own lives.

When the shepherd loses one from his flock of one hundred sheep, he leaves the ninety-nine in the open country to go search for the stray. Finding it, he calls his friends and neighbors to rejoice with him. Jesus says, "I tell you that in the same way there will be more rejoicing in heaven over one sinner who repents than over ninety-nine righteous persons who do not need to repent" (Luke 15:7).

When the woman with ten silver coins loses one, she sweeps her house and searches until she finds it. Then she too calls her neighbors to rejoice with her.

Finally, Luke records the familiar parable of the prodigal son, who after squandering his inheritance in wild living, comes to his senses and returns home to the welcoming arms of a joyful, forgiving father. Excitedly this man calls for a celebration because his son, whom he thought was dead, "is alive again; he was lost and is found" (Luke 15:32). In the same way, our heavenly Father welcomes all prodigals into his arms and into his kingdom.

The following stories tell of miracles in which the lost are found. As you read them, remember that God delights in showing us his treasures. Open your eyes and your heart to him. Allow him to show you lovingkindness—and then rejoice.

LOST IN VIETNAM

As Ann Fraser discovered, sometimes you have to lose something precious to you before you find something that is even more precious.[1]

Twenty-five years ago my husband, Ken, was the center of my life. Everything I did was to please him. My every thought was how I could make him happy. He was my reason for living.

One bleak winter day in 1972, however, my world collapsed. Ken had been away, in Southeast Asia, for eight months, and my arms ached to hold him close. We had been planning a reunion in two weeks, a second honeymoon. Then I received the shocking news that his airplane had been shot down somewhere over North Vietnam.

The night the Air Force officials told me he was missing in action, I cried until there was no strength left in me. Missing in action. I was plagued with thoughts of Ken lying in a rotting jungle thicket. Was his body burned? Broken? Was he dead or alive? It was such agony—wondering and not knowing. I was afraid to hope and unable to stop hoping.

My mother's pastor, Henry Lyon, came to my house and prayed, asking God to keep Ken alive. "Lord, hear him," I wanted to shout. "Right now I don't have the kind of faith to pray like that. I want to believe. Help me believe. Find Ken for me, God." I had been brought up to go to church, but now as I faced this crisis, I realized my faith was very shallow. I didn't know how I could make it without Ken. I cried and cried, and cried some more—agonizing over my husband, agonizing over my future.

Two days later an officer from the casualty center in Texas called. "Mrs. Fraser, your husband is alive." I sank to the floor, clutching the kitchen phone so tightly my knuckles turned white. He went on to tell me that Ken had been captured. In North Vietnam he and four other prisoners had been paraded before a group of foreign newsmen. They had taken pictures, and Ken had been identified. Alive! Standing on two legs! Maybe God was as real as the pastor said. He had graciously answered our prayer. I felt as though the dead had been raised.

That night I wrote in my journal: "Such joy just to know he is alive and still somewhere in this world. Never thought I'd be happy he is a POW (Prisoner of War). But life—his life—is so precious and God is so good to let him live. "

To keep busy, I threw myself into projects—volunteering as a Red Cross worker, teaching young girls at church, selling bracelets with POW names on them. I made speeches and did whatever I could to keep the public aware of the plight of the POWs and MIAs (Missing In Action).

Life magazine published a picture of Ken—a full color page—and I couldn't stop looking at it. I read the sadness in his eyes and wanted to share his pain. His left arm was in a cast. What did that mean? And what other injuries did he have? I worried. I prayed. I wished him home, at my side—to fill the void in my heart.

As the war escalated, I prayed harder. I received several hundred letters from people who were wearing bracelets with Ken's name on them. Many told me they were praying for Ken.

Four months after his capture, I got my first letter from my husband. What joy! Many of my letters to him had been returned. Through the long summer months I sent him packages of coffee, gum, freeze-dried foods, hard candies. Were they getting through? I didn't know.

I heard the wife of an MIA speak at the base chapel—how she had peace and was trusting God no matter what. Why couldn't I trust God like that? What did I lack? I wondered.

The three children and I just went through the motions of the Christmas holidays, which seemed meaningless without Ken. Little Christie kept wanting to go to the airport just in case Daddy had come home. My New Year's prayer was that the war would end that year and that Ken would come home. If he did, everything would be fine.

And in March 1973 we got the good news. Peace talks had been successful. Prisoners would be coming home—but I didn't dare really believe it until Ken was safely on U.S. soil. Our three children nearly exploded with excitement as we drove to Montgomery, Alabama, two months later to meet him. Friends and relatives, cheers and banners greeted him. What a celebration!

Ken filled me in on his thirteen months in a Hanoi prison. The tale was heartbreaking, but he was able to see and appreciate some bright spots, some small graces. After his capture, while in solitary confinement, he had prayed that somehow I would find out that he was alive. God had honored that prayer. And he and his fellow prisoners had been allowed to have a Bible for Sunday worship.

We began to pick up the pieces of our lives after Ken came home. First, doctors performed corrective surgery on his left arm. We found ourselves showered with gifts, including a car, because of Ken's return as a war hero. We were flown to the White House to join other returning POWs in a reception hosted by President Nixon. When Ken was transferred to Eglin Air Force Base in Florida, we were able to buy our first house.

Our family was back together. We were "set" for the future, but something vital was still missing. Both Ken and I sensed this, though we did not know what it was. We visited several churches and were finally drawn back to one where people seemed to know God personally and where we felt loved.

One November morning, while sitting in a blue-cushioned pew in that church, I remembered the MIA officer's wife who had spoken to us in the base chapel months before. She had shown the same kind of love I saw in these people. She had had peace. Now as I listened to the sermon, I realized for the first time that I had never made Jesus Christ Lord of my life. In a simple prayer of commitment, I surrendered everything I was and had to him.

While I didn't understand it, I was experiencing a second miracle that year. I found real peace, the kind I had been looking for while Ken had been missing, the peace that had eluded me even after he was back at my side. The same week Ken, too, turned his life over to Christ.

Ken is no longer the center of my life, and I am no longer the center of his. Jesus has filled the "something vital" that was missing from both of our lives. Previously we had known *about* him; now we knew him personally. And we, who were both "lost" in a sense, were found.

Sometimes we are sure that a certain "find" will make everything all right, but that's not necessarily true. Ann found something more vital than her lost husband—a personal relationship with God.

FINDING MY FATHER

Someone growing up in a family with a poor role model in a dad may have a hard time identifying with a loving heavenly Father. You feel lost, out of place. This is a story of one woman who discovered, even late in her life, that God had been there all along for her.

Callie tells her story:

Have you ever felt alone even while living in a family? Lost? As if you didn't quite belong but you didn't know why? That is exactly how I felt. Then one day, curled up on the couch daydreaming, I said to my Mom, "I just had the crazy thought that I remember the day you and Dad married."

In a tight voice, she responded, "Callie, that's because you were there that day. You were five years old when we married. Your birth father had mistreated us, and I came home to live with your grandmother and granddad."

She closed the conversation firmly and never mentioned it again. A couple of years later, while rummaging in Mom's closet, I opened a shirt box and found an adoption certificate giving the name of my real father, my real birth name. Though my dad now had a name, for me he still had no face.

I now understood why I had felt alone—not quite part of this family. I loved my mom and little sister dearly, but my stepdad—who had legally adopted me—was often distant, unapproving, and critical toward me. When he drank, his violent temper was unpredictable, and I was afraid of and intimidated by him.

As I grew up, tensions increased between my stepfather and me. Emotionally I moved away from home, reaching out to friends and their families for a sense of family and belonging.

Once in college, I was popular and happy, not very aware of "father issues." Home from college on the warm summer morning of my eighteenth birthday, I got a call from a relative I didn't know. "Happy birthday, Callie. Would you like to meet your father?" She reminded me that I was now legally old enough to make a choice to see him. Of course, I wanted to.

We arranged a meeting place on the far end of town. When I arrived, I knew him immediately—recognizing myself in him. His deep blue eyes, his personality, his ways—all a missing part of me. In our hour-long visit, he assured me Mom was a very good woman and their marriage failure had been totally his fault. He went on to tell me that he had remarried and had a daughter Susan, whom he hoped I would someday get to know. He asked only that I not come into his family and then decide to drop it and hurt Susan. I could understand his concern. We agreed to see each other again. It was a good meeting, though deeply emotional for me.

When I got home, my mother was very upset. Someone who had seen us together had called her. I was given a choice—to get out immediately or to sign a letter already prepared saying I would not pursue a relationship with my father. I signed the letter and sent it to my father, and I did not hear from him again.

While in graduate school I met and married a very special man. Secure in my marriage, I began to think about my father again.

Years later, as my mother was dying of cancer, I asked her, "Mom, it is important that you be clear with God. Have you forgiven everyone who has hurt you—even my dad?"

"Yes," she replied. "I have forgiven your father and all others." A month later she died.

Six years after that, my husband and I were on vacation. When we passed through my hometown in Virginia, I decided on the spur of the moment to try to learn if anyone might know something about my dad. For various reasons I thought he was dead. But several phone calls to relatives told me I was wrong. My father was still alive, living in New England with his wife, daughter, and son-in-law. He had recently had a stroke but was home from the hospital.

We were actually heading for Vermont, and we would be passing through my dad's town the next day. My husband, Jack, and I started praying that I would be able to connect with him.

When I phoned the house where my father was living, Susan's husband, Rick, answered. I asked for my father, John, by name and told Rick I was John's daughter by a previous marriage.

"Does your wife know I even exist?" I asked. "I don't want to cause any hurt in your family."

"Yes, we know all about you, Callie."

"I'd like to see my father . . . tomorrow . . . on our way north."

He checked with others and said, "Dad will be home alone with his physical therapist tomorrow afternoon. That will be a good time to visit."

That evening an earthquake of emotion erupted inside me as I contemplated the next day's visit.

As we drove up to the house the next afternoon, I was counting on my husband going in with me for emotional support. But he has been disabled by polio, and when we saw the house, I knew I could not get his wheelchair up the long flight of stairs to the door. I would have to make this visit alone while he sat in the car and prayed for me.

Inside I found a slender, silver-haired man sitting quietly. One side of his mouth drooped, and he was unable to speak. But the piercing, deep blue eyes were unchanged.

"Dad, I'm Callie, your other daughter," I said, reaching for his hand. Tears welled up in his eyes. I told him that I had often found it difficult not having my own father with me. I missed him. I told him that knowing Jesus had helped me through lonely times.

My dad was unable to utter a single word of response to me.

"Are you glad I came, Dad?" I finally asked.

"Yes, yes," he nodded while huge tears spilled from his eyes.

"Dad, before Mom died she wanted to be right with God, and she forgave you everything."

Laying his head on my shoulder, he sobbed. At that moment, his family walked in. They were cordial. I invited Susan and her husband to join Jack and me for dinner that night.

At the restaurant I admitted to Susan, "I didn't know if you knew I existed."

"Oh, yes, Callie. Daddy had someone watching out for you, and he always shared each bit of news he would get, so that if we ever met, we would not be strangers."

It was hard to believe! All those years I had felt an empty place in me where a father's love should have been, and yet my dad had not forgotten me. He had someone watching out for me, reporting all the details of my life to him. He had known about my graduation from college, about my marriage to Jack, a doctor.

That night I wept and wept in my husband's arms, experiencing a kaleidoscope of emotions. Joy at seeing my dad. Joy that he had received me. Agony over not being able to hear his voice say "I love you." Feeling sorrow that I had waited too long! Wondering if I should have tried to contact him earlier.

As we entered Vermont the next day, we stopped at an antique shop where I browsed while Jack napped in the car. I had been there before, but had never gone into one dark room off to the right, full of tapestries. Now I felt almost compelled to check it out. Inside, my eyes fastened onto a tattered and grayed cross-stitch wall hanging, dated 1830, that contained this saying:

Love the Lord and He will be a tender Father to thee.

I knew this message was just for me—and perfectly timed. In earlier years, before I knew my earthly father had any interest in me, I had been pitifully unable to identify with a heavenly Father's love. God wanted me to know that he—God himself—had been a tender loving Father to me all my years, and that he would always be the one who would watch over me.

It was as though all the whispered prayers I had carried in my heart since I was a little girl were now answered.

Standing there, in tears, I began to close the door on the fears, the mistrusts, and the hurts of the past.

I sensed I would not see my earthly father again. And two months later I learned that he had died. When I got the news, I closed my eyes and saw that old tattered cloth, "Love the Lord and He will be a tender Father to thee." A little thing, you may say, but a great miracle that the God of all creation, in his infinite compassion, reaches down, cuts across the ages, and intervenes on behalf of one hurt little child—his child.

If you have ever come to the place where you really know God's tender loving heart toward you, you will understand.

Lost but found.

FINDING A SPECIAL LOST RING

God is certainly more interested in people than things, but he does care about possessions that are precious to us. Our daughter Sherry, married and living in Copenhagen, told us about a disarming burglary in their fifth-floor walk-up apartment.

As I climbed the last stairs, I was puzzled to see small wooden pieces strewn around the entryway. Then I saw that our entry door hung partially open. *Thieves!*

A neighbor went inside with me. The intruder had left, but the damage was done—drawers pulled out and papers scattered everywhere. It looked as though a tornado had blown through. Strewn across a chair lay pieces of our favorite antique wall cabinet, carved up in an attempt to pry open a small locked drawer. Strangers had been through every bit of our personal possessions. Inside I cried, "God help us, and God help us to forgive."

I dialed the police, then my husband, Kim. Clearing a path to the living room couch, I sat down to wait for them to arrive. "It was a clean job," the policeman said. "They take the valuables that are easy to carry and that they can sell for quick cash."

When we finished the inventory, we were missing one U.S. passport, a portable CD player, some cash, and my husband's gold wedding band—inscribed with my name, Sherry, and our wedding day, 26–7–87.

The passport and the CD player could be replaced, we decided. And the money was God's anyway, being the tithe we had set aside. But what really upset us was the loss of the wedding ring, which could not be replaced.

Later that night, we put the situation in God's hands. "Most of all, Lord, please bring back the ring," we prayed in agreement.

Weeks went by, and we were eventually able to let go of the fear of having someone ransack our apartment. We were even able to forgive the intruder.

We continued to pray for the ring to be returned, though the police gave us little hope of ever finding it. Months passed. Then one Friday afternoon I received a phone call from the police in Roskilde, a small city about thirty miles away. "We have found a ring that matches the description in the report from the robbery. Can you verify this information?"

He described it perfectly—the American name Sherry and the date inscribed inside. I cried excitedly, "Yes, that's it!" The ring had been found on a patient at the mental hospital. The police determined he was probably the third or fourth person to have it, though he did not explain how or why he made that judgment.

Two days later a little brown envelope arrived in the mail; the lost had been returned. I began jumping up and down, rejoicing over the found ring but also thanking God for our miracle answer to prayer.

Sometimes all we can do is release our "losses" to God's care and continue to pray.

LOST BUT FOUND

After her husband, Len, died, Ruth Friesen drove her two grandchildren to Canada to visit her relatives. When she returned home her driveway was covered with pine needles and cones. Sweeping them up was traditionally Len's job—now it was left to her. Because rain was predicted, she decided to tackle the chore before unpacking.

She didn't take time to change her clothes, but she took off her diamond watch and wedding rings, not wanting dust and dirt to get on them. After sweeping the driveway, she drove to a nearby fast-food restaurant for a hamburger. Back home, she unpacked her suitcase and worked in her flower garden, filling two bags of garbage from the beds.

Two days later she could not remember where she had put her rings and watch. They had disappeared. She prayed particularly about retrieving the wedding rings, which Len had given to her forty-seven years ago. Now that he was gone, their loss seemed traumatically significant.

"We'll pray, Mom, and you'll get them back," her two daughters assured her. "You will find your rings," her sister in Canada also responded when she called.

Four nights later, at 12:30 A.M., Ruth gasped. She suddenly remembered—she had put the jewelry on the car, and then she had driven off to the restaurant. Just before dawn, when she could endure waiting no longer, she grabbed a flashlight and went out to search, all along the driveway and front curb.

No rings. No watch.

She asked her neighbors and their children. No one had seen them. She called the police and insurance company. "Forget about them, lady. You won't get them back," an agent told her.

She had a choice, to believe the insurance company and forget about the rings, or to believe nothing was impossible to her God; he could find them for her.

She made one final effort to do what she could to rustle up the rings; she ran an ad in the daily newspaper. No response.

And then the rings "came to her." When a community flier was thrown at her door, she picked it up. Though she usually tossed these in the trash, she decided to glance through the lost and found column. There an ad caught her eye: "Lady's wedding rings found. Identify."

She called the phone number. After she described them, the man said, "They're yours alright. Come and get them."

"Apparently they had flipped off my car a long block from my home as I rounded the corner. They'd been run over by a car and were thrown into the sand against the curb. The young man was out walking at sunset when they glistened, catching his attention. God heard our prayers for the rings and had someone find them who would advertise and return them," Ruth said.

Ruth gave the man a gift certificate for dinner for two at the country club and a reward check—which he had not asked for. The man was delighted—the certificate coming just in time for his wedding anniversary.

Persistent prayer paid off, aided by Ruth's unfailing faith that what was precious to her would be found. Like the woman in Luke 15, she called her friends to share her good news!

FOUND BY AN ANGEL

In this final lost and found miracle story, I build a bridge to my next topic, "Miracles of Angelic Intervention." Sandra Wezowicz was amazed at how God answered her prayer for protection of her lost possession. She tells the story in her words:

Early on a Thursday morning, I pulled into the local service station to get some gas. I was preoccupied and in a hurry. The day's to-do list was longer than the day itself. I eased up to the first pump, turned off the ignition, and, as if on automatic pilot, grabbed the first nozzle for super unleaded gas, lifted the lever, and began to pump. Nothing came out. Then my eye caught the new sign, "Please Prepay."

I grabbed my wallet out of my purse on the front seat, dashed in, and handed the young woman at the cash register a ten dollar bill. I pumped my gas and went on my way.

Several miles down the busy road I gasped with horror as I remembered that I had left my wallet on the roof of the car! I immediately pulled over, hoping against hope that my wallet might still be there. But there was no wallet.

I did not have much money in the wallet, though I did have five credit cards, my driver's license, photos, and other personal stuff. I felt sick to lose all of them.

With great fervency, I cried out, "O God, help me! Please put an angel on my wallet."

Suddenly and, I have to admit, with great surprise, a feeling of incredible peace flooded through me. I drove to my destination and called my husband with the news. I hated to admit my stupidity and carelessness. His response was practical: "Call the bank and credit card companies and cancel the cards."

"But honey," I protested, "I just know the Lord has an angel on it."

"Fine, but please cancel the cards anyway."

Hanging up, I made that my first priority of business. The next day, Friday, I spent replacing my driver's license and looking for a new wallet. I figured I might as well enjoy the weekend and wait until Monday to work on replacing the cards. On Sunday afternoon I attended a musical concert with some of my friends. Afterwards, when I walked into the house, my husband had good news. "Sandy, your wallet is on the kitchen counter. Donna"—the music teacher who used to teach with me—"brought it over. One of her neighbors found it."

I called Donna to thank her and ask for a few details. She explained that an older, Hispanic couple living in the next apartment found the wallet early Thursday morning while out walking. When they showed her the wallet, Donna told them she knew me and would return it.

I was overjoyed. On Monday morning I went to the florist and ordered a bud vase of roses. I wanted to thank them in person. I drove to the complex, found their apartment, and knocked on the door. An older woman with a kind face opened the door. I knew her English wasn't very good, so I spoke simply and with hand gestures. "Thank you," I said, showing her my wallet. "I'm Sandy and these are for you." After I handed her the flowers, I pointed toward heaven, "I prayed and asked Jesus to send an angel to find my wallet."

She gasped, put her hand over her heart, and whispered, "My husband, he find it. His name is Angel!"

Sometimes miracles come in such unexpected ways that we who are on the receiving end stand back in amazement and exclaim, "God did it! He did it just for me." We feel like throwing a party—like the woman in Luke 15 who found her lost coin, like the father whose lost son returned home.

God cares about our lost—people and things!

Praying the Scriptures
FOUND BY GOD

The angel of the Lord *found Hagar near a spring in the desert. . . .*

Genesis 16:7

Again, the kingdom of heaven is like a merchant looking for fine pearls. When he found one of great value, he went away and sold everything he had and bought it.

Matthew 13:45–46

For the Son of Man came to seek and to save what was lost.

Luke 19:10

And this is the will of him who sent me, that I shall lose none of all that he has given me, but raise them up at the last day. For the Father's will is that everyone who looks to the Son and believes in him shall have eternal life, and I will raise him up at the last day.

John 6:39–40

PART FIVE

Miracles of Angelic Intervention

See, I am sending an angel ahead of you to guard you along the way.

EXODUS 23:20

The angels are part of God's ingenious provision for us. Because they are so passionately in love with God, the angels are perfectly conformed to his will. Whatever he tells them to do they do. Whoever he loves, they can't help but love. Because God cares for us so deeply, we can claim the wonderful friendship of angels.

ANN SPANGLER[1]

God has given us the gift of angels to watch over and protect us. What are angels? The word "angel" is derived from a Greek term meaning "messenger"; it appears nearly two hundred times in the New Testament. Angels are supernatural beings that exist in the heavenlies, serving both as *messengers* from God and *protectors* of his children. Angels are in ceaseless service to God. According to Billy Graham, angels "are God's messengers whose chief business is to carry out his orders in the world."[2]

Psalm 91 promises angelic protection for those who have made the Lord their dwelling place; God will command his angels over us (Psalm 91:9–13). We may ask God to send angels to protect us, but let's be cautious about *demanding* angels for ourselves. What we believe must be grounded in the Bible.

Angels figured big in Jesus' life. The angel Gabriel told the Virgin Mary she would bear the Christ child. Angels heralded his birth. They ministered to him after the devil tempted him on the high mountain. An angel declared the joyous news of the resurrection to the women who came to the tomb. When the Son of man returns in all his glory, the holy angels will come with him.

And angels played a large role in the advancement of the early church. An angel freed Peter from prison while an intense prayer meeting was in session at the home of John Mark's mother. An angel directed Cornelius to find a man (Peter) who would lead him to salvation. Philip the evangelist was directed by an angel to go to the desert road that led from Jerusalem to Gaza to explain the Gospel to an Ethiopian.

The Bible regularly speaks of angels as real spiritual beings. One of my favorite biblical angel stories is in the Old Testament. The prophet Elisha knew God had his angels watching over him, but his servant was not as aware of the heavenly forces. That servant became alarmed when an infantry approached their city, intent on capturing Elisha.

The prophet assured him, "Those who are with us are more than those who are with them." When Elisha asked God to open the servant's eyes, the man saw into the invisible realm—a hillside host of horses and chariots of fire. "God's angelic strike-force," Dick Eastman calls them.[3] Through the word of Elisha, the enemy was struck with blindness, and the prophet led them directly into the city of Samaria (see 2 Kings 6:14–20).

I have mentioned angels as being messengers of God, but the Bible indicates that there are good angels and evil angels—God's angels and Satan's angels. It describes the long ago war in heaven in which Lucifer, one of the most beautiful of all created heavenly beings, rebelled against God and took with him myriads of angels who chose to deny the authority of God.

Billy Graham writes on this:

> Lucifer, the son of the morning, was created, as were all angels, for the purpose of glorifying God. However, instead of serving God and praising Him forever, Satan desired to rule over heaven and creation in the place of God. He wanted supreme authority! Lucifer said (Isaiah 14), "I will ascend into heaven." "I will exalt my throne above the stars of God." "I will be like the most high."
>
> Lucifer became Satan, the devil, the author of sin; and it is sin that has always deceived, disturbed, betrayed, depraved and destroyed all that it has touched.[4]

Beware of any angel experience that does not line up with the word of God. Many New Age teachings are deceiving even Christians. "Satan himself masquerades as an angel of light" (2 Corinthians 11:14). False religions and philosophies with angel appearances focus on "self" or "I," as did Lucifer. Angels of God point people to God.

The Bible teaches that angels are spirits, but there are instances in the Bible where they take on visible bodies or human manifestations. Sometimes God sends angels in the form of persons; other times he chooses to let mere mortals view beings that are obviously otherworldly. Some people have heard angels. Others have never seen or heard them, but have sensed that in answer to their prayers, God sent angels to rescue them from sudden danger.

As you read this next group of stories, allow God to open your eyes to the reality of his angels, who keep watch over you—whether you see them or not.

A VISION OF ANGELS

Zee Jones did not know how she would ever emotionally handle the death of one of her parents. In her own words she tells what happened when the dreaded day finally came.

As a young woman, on January 16, 1959, in a hospital in Creston, British Columbia, I stood at the bedside of my father, Harry Scott. Four days earlier he had suffered a severe heart attack.

My oldest brother, Blair, was reading Scripture to Dad. Mother was standing on the other side of his bed. Very heavily sedated, he was unable to talk to us, but Blair asked him to raise his eyebrows if he could hear the reading. Yes, he could.

Dad was in a corner room, with no exit at this end of the hall. As Blair was reading aloud Psalm 23, I suddenly heard music behind me. I turned around to see where it was coming from. As I did, an amazing thing happened. The wall opened up, and I saw with my own eyes a choir of angels in white robes singing a gospel song I recognized from church, "Coming home, coming home. . . . Open wide your arms of love. Lord, I'm coming home." Their voices were beautiful.

I turned back around to look at Dad. Did he see them too? Just then he opened his eyes, and a look of ecstasy came upon his face. Then he closed his eyes and gave a little gasp, and he was gone—gone home to his Lord. The angels must have come for him, transporting my dad into the very presence of God.

Neither my mother nor my brother heard or saw the angels, but I did and so did my dad. This was God's special grace to me. I couldn't even mourn my dad's passing after this exhilarating experience. It was one of the greatest highlights of my life. I have had no fear or dread of death since then.

The Bible tells us we are "carried by angels" into heaven (see Luke 16:22). What comfort for Christians to know that mighty angels escort us to our eternal home.

WARRING ANGELS

Ruthie Mason was startled by a crazy thought that flashed through her head as the Sunday night service was ending. *Your house is being robbed.* She and Sid had been in Portland, Oregon, for the weekend and would be returning home to Salem as soon as church was over. She picks up the story:

I tried to dismiss the awful thought. The Salem newspapers had reported frequent house burglaries, but not in our neighborhood. Perhaps it was the Holy Spirit alerting me to pray. "Lord, we've lived in that house for thirty years. If our house is being robbed, please send an angel—no, Lord, send a warring angel—to frighten the burglar off." Then I began quoting Scriptures, praying for protection: "No evil will come near our dwelling place. . . . No weapon formed against us shall prosper. . . ."

On the fifty-minute drive back home, I finally admitted to my husband, "Dear, I have the strangest feeling our home was broken into tonight."

"That is really odd," he replied. "So did I."

Rounding the corner to our home, Sid pushed the automatic garage door opener. Lights came on, and we immediately saw that the frame door to the garage was kicked in, as was the door into the backyard.

I lingered in the locked car while Sid went in to investigate. He found the glass patio door smashed; glass lay all over the kitchen floor and had been tracked onto the dining room carpet. But no one seemed to be inside the house or garage.

When I went in, I surveyed the scene. The silver tea service and silver candelabra were sitting on the buffet. Sterling silverware, pulled from the drawers, was lying on the dining table. All my jewelry had been thrown into the center of our bed. On the corner of the dresser lay a hammer, obviously used to smash the patio door. Strangely, beside the hammer was a new watch still in its box, removed from a dresser drawer. Things were surely in a mess, but it wasn't immediately obvious that valuables were missing.

A policeman arrived, and we showed him through the house. In a bedroom my husband noticed a pillow lying on the floor without a pillow slip. "I wonder why a pillow slip is missing," he mentioned.

"That's the first thing a burglar gets so he can use it to stash what he's going to take away," he told us. "With so many of the drawers in the house left open, I'm sure you may later remember other things you are missing. Take your time to make your report for the police and insurance company. Be sure to include everything missing."

That night Sid nailed our long redwood picnic table over our patio door and we tried to sleep. I prayed for safety and peace, though we didn't get much rest.

The next day the police officer returned. "Did you find a lot of missing things?" he asked us.

"No, we haven't. As far as we can tell nothing is missing—nothing. Not even my good gold jewelry," I replied.

He looked around at my china, silver, and gold vases. "With all these beautiful things, I don't understand why you weren't robbed blind. Something obviously frightened away the intruder. He left in a hurry."

Two houses in Ruthie's neighborhood were robbed that night, but hers was spared. She is sure that God answered her specific prayer, that God sent a warring angel of protection to frighten away a burglar. Ruthie's story reminds me of a line by Thomas Watson: "The angel fetched Peter out of prison, but it was prayer that fetched the angel."

ANGELS RESCUE RECREATIONAL VEHICLE

In 1978 I myself asked God for an angelic intervention—a prayer he miraculously answered.

On a Friday afternoon my friend Lib and I were driving from Miami back home to Titusville, Florida. We still had another one hundred miles to go. I had been visiting my aunt, who had loaded my car with house plants because she was moving north and didn't want to take them with her.

That same afternoon my husband, LeRoy, was driving this same four-lane freeway but in the opposite direction, with our pastor and several other men going south for a weekend retreat. Somewhere on the busy divided highway we might see their recreational vehicle whiz by. Highly unlikely, I decided. Nevertheless, I looked at my watch and said, "Let's just keep our eye out, Lib. Wouldn't it be funny if we did see them?"

I kept driving. A few minutes later I glanced across the freeway and saw a Winnebago RV rolling south.

"Look Lib! I think I recognized LeRoy driving that RV." But I also noticed that the vehicle seemed to be in trouble. Black smoke was pouring out the back end. "There's no way we can go after them," I said. "I don't know how far it is to the next turnaround. Let's ask God to give them wisdom and to send angels to protect them."

We prayed for a while, telling God we trusted him to send whatever help LeRoy needed—including angels. I felt at peace as we drove toward home. Off and on as I thought about my husband that weekend, I would pray, but not with anxiety.

As soon as LeRoy walked in the door from the retreat, he gave me a hug and said, "Hey, we must have had an angel or two holding us up for some miles on our way down to the ranch."

"I know," I replied. "Lib and I prayed and asked the Lord to surround you with them."

"Really?"

Then he told me his story, "I was driving the RV when I sensed I was losing control over the steering. I told the men I was stopping the Winnebago to check it out. I pulled over and they got out. I drove forward, and the guys who were looking underneath it said everything looked okay. Then I told them to stand clear so I could back up. When I put the RV in reverse and released the brake, the right front wheel assembly, including the axle, twisted off. The vehicle fell on top of the wheel. We had to get a wrecker and call for a friend to bring us a car so we could get to the retreat in time for supper."

None of the men had seen the smoke bellowing out. None suspected trouble. But my husband, a mechanical engineer, knew from the way the vehicle steered that something was wrong. God does intervene.

Had the prayers Lib and I prayed been the connecting link? We all agreed God sent angels, though we have no proof. God's angels are present even when we don't see them.

THE NIGHT THE ANGELS SANG

October 1975. Beirut, Lebanon. War was raging on every side, and finally right in the neighborhood where Americans Esther and Bill Ilnisky lived. For their denomination, they were in charge of nine university campus ministries in Beirut.

Though the country was in a crisis, Esther and Bill had not stopped their ministry. They were seeing great spiritual growth among the college students, especially as a result of Esther's work as director of The Solid Rock, a musical group that presented the Gospel in song.

Escalated street battles were torching fires in the downtown hotel and apartment district. Schools and banks were closed. Garbage had not been collected in weeks. Often snipers shot those who came to carry away the dead, so bodies were sometimes left in the streets. The city had been under curfew for two months. The United States ambassador had advised all Americans to leave Beirut.

The Ilnisky family had been missionaries in Lebanon for six years and kept believing things would improve. But on this night as Esther peered through large glass windows in her fifth-story apartment less than a block from the Mediterranean, she saw smoke being wind-blown toward her area of town. Sniper, machine gun, and rocket battles raged. In moments their own building was under attack.

Esther tells the rest of the story herself:

Our eleven-year-old daughter, Sarah, and I crawled into a hallway, the only safe place in our apartment. Bill was in our bedroom trying to pull down some wooden shutters.

Sarah and I huddled together while bullets ricocheted off our brick building. As I prayed, I couldn't help but remember friends back in Orlando who had promised to pray and fast for us during this our second tour of duty in

Lebanon. "Your names will be lifted before the throne of God daily," one had promised.

Suddenly the sound of crunching, shattering glass faded as a sweet crescendo of music penetrated my ears. At close range a choir was singing our names—Bill's, Sarah's, and mine. I opened my eyes but saw no one. Still a host of voices, in a magnificent chorus, continued singing our names in glorious harmony. "Angels," I said in a half whisper. Yes, they were blended together in concert. I knew the Lord heard them too.

Then, as if redirecting themselves to another audience, their tone quality became masterful, authoritative. It was as though every force of evil had to hear them and be dispelled.

As I sat there, caught up in the ecstasy of the moment, I suddenly remembered a missionary prayer conference we had attended a few months earlier. Our group had studied Daniel 10—the account of the battle between the Prince of Persia (Satan's angel) and God's angels. Through a prophetic message from the Holy Spirit, we had understood that the role of angels in our work and lives would take on a new dimension—because tragic days were coming.

Now we were experiencing it. I thought of my mother and father, who had taught me as a little girl that God had his angels watching over me. Two verses from the Psalms leaped to memory and burst into reality for me. "For he shall give his angels charge over thee, to keep thee in all thy ways. They shall bear thee up in their hands, lest thou dash thy foot against a stone" (Psalm 91: 11–12 KJV).

Once again the angel voices came to me in sweetly flowing tones, ministering personally, like a mother singing a lullaby to a restless baby. As they sang, God's peace flooded every fiber of my being.

Even with the stench of death around us, with the thud of bullets hitting only a few yards away, and with billowing pillars of fire and smoke spiraling above the city, I was filled with God's abiding peace. And it stayed with me through the next harrowing days.

Though Satan's emissaries might be surrounding the country of war-torn Lebanon, the prayers of the believers were getting through. God's angels had come to intervene.

Soon after this attack, the Ilnisky family left Lebanon and returned to Florida. Today they live in West Palm Beach, where Bill pastors a large church. Esther is director of Esther Network International, which mobilizes children around the world to pray for the needs of the world.

How comforting to know God sends angels to minister to us in the most frightening times of our lives. They even know our names. For this family the key factor was that friends back home were continually praying for their safety. Prayer and miracles are closely intertwined, even when angels are needed on the scene.

GUIDED BY ANGELS

Sandy Baur will never know if the two Koreans who came to her aid were angels or just God-sent humans. To her it doesn't really matter. Trying to find the right bus in a foreign country, unable to communicate because of the language barrier—she needed a miracle.

In autumn 1994 Sandy attended a conference in Seoul, South Korea. With the event behind her, she decided to take a side trip; she would catch a bus to the Osan Air Force Base to see Pete, her daughter's fiancé. Pete had told her she could get a bus that would take her almost to the door of his base.

But at the bus terminal, the agents didn't know English, and she couldn't speak their language. After a lot of head shaking, she finally figured out she was at the wrong bus terminal. A businessman standing nearby spoke a few words of English, and he phoned a friend to see if he could give Sandy directions. But once on the phone, the conversation

—with someone whose English was not coherent—left Sandy more confused than ever.

"Lord, please help me! I don't know what to do," she prayed.

Almost immediately a Korean woman in her mid-fifties appeared on one side of her, and a young man in his twenties approached her on the other side. They spoke very little English but took hold of her by both arms and said in very broken English, "Come with us."

It puzzled her because they didn't even seem to know one another. Yet both seemed to know where she wanted to go. Did they overhear her mention the Air Force base in her phone conversation? Their own English was so poor, she doubted it.

With utter trust—she sensed God had sent them to help her—she let them lead her. The three of them walked out of the station and underground until they came to the correct subway. The Koreans bought three tickets and boarded the train with her. Then, at the "right time," they ushered her off. After walking four blocks, still holding tightly to her arms, the trio arrived at the other bus terminal.

"Korean bus terminals can be compared to Chicago's O'Hare airport at Christmastime," Sandy says.

After saying something in Korean to the young man, the woman seemed to disappear. The man went up to the counter and bought a ticket. Then the woman returned, carrying a small brown bag.

The two strangers waited with Sandy until the right bus came. The man handed Sandy a ticket; the woman handed her the brown sack. After her companions spoke to the bus driver, Sandy boarded the bus. Her smiling Korean benefactors waited beside the bus at least twenty minutes, until it pulled out of the station. They were still waving as Sandy took one last look back.

Sandy opened the sack the woman had given her. Inside was a hamburger, French fries, and a Coke—appropriately American food. The bus ride was uneventful. When she got off, she had only two blocks to walk to meet Pete.

Sandy remains puzzled about the two "angels" who came to her aid. They paid for everything along her journey. She did not know their names and has no idea where they came from. They guided her through the crowded streets, knowing exactly where she needed to go and anticipating her hunger.

Whoever they were, it was obvious that God knew her dilemma. To a visitor in a strange land he sent strangers to help her find her way.

ANGELS WATCHING OVER ME

Theata Frenzel thought she had reached the end of her rope in 1979. She had lost her husband through divorce and her dad through death. Though she had occasionally attended church, she says she was "not acquainted personally with Jesus as Lord." But God allowed a miraculous intervention to draw her into her heavenly Father's arms.

She tells what happened:

That devastating year I told God, "I don't want to live. I have nothing to live for."

A few weeks later, on January 8, 1980, I was driving into Beaumont, Texas, to go to work. About five miles from my home I got off the interstate to avoid a traffic pile-up. After about three miles, I decided to get back on the freeway. As I did so, I was hit from the rear, lost control of my car, and shot across two lanes of traffic. I looked up and saw an eighteen wheeler heading straight toward me. I cried out to God, "My life is yours, Lord. Whatever your will is for me, I accept it. Please keep others from being hurt."

My car hit the rear tires of the truck, sending me back across the lanes of traffic I had just traversed. My car rolled over three times, stopping upside down. I thought the car was on fire, though the "smoke" I smelled was really exhaust.

I was unable to get out the driver's side, so I scooted over to the passenger's side. I was upside down, but I could still use my feet to push the door open. When it did, glass shattered everywhere. I started to run—and then fainted.

When I opened my eyes, I was lying by the side of the road. A man with brownish red hair and a beard was holding my hand, speaking words of comfort. Every time I asked how my face, hands, or feet were, he told me I was going to be okay. I was positive I was bleeding profusely, but he assured me it was just misting rain.

When the ambulance arrived, the kind man holding my hand said, "I will never leave you or forsake you. I will be with you at the hospital. Everything is going to be fine."

I overheard a lady tell the officer that the truck was probably going seventy miles an hour when we collided. Even so, I had no significant injuries, and doctors sent me home to rest and recover from the trauma.

While recuperating, I began to read my Bible with intense hunger. Since that man had stayed at my side, holding my hand, after I had passed out, Jesus had seemed so real to me.

I made numerous phone calls trying to find the stranger. But the ambulance driver said he had not seen him. Nor the wrecker driver. Nor even the police officer who was at the scene.

Was he an angel? Or did I have a visitation from Jesus himself? Was I healed at the scene? Was my life spared for a purpose? I don't know who my visitor was. I only know God saved my life, and I am glad.

A deep change came within me as a result of my accident. I wanted to live. Today I am happily married, and my husband and I have a ministry of helping others who have lost all hope and want to die as I once did.

Sometimes when we think there is no reason to live, God intervenes to bring us back to reality. Yes, there is a reason, a hope, a destiny for us. And he may use a miracle to show us his love, care, and concern. We in turn can then shower it on others—as Theata now does.

ANGELS IN CRISIS TIMES

Doctors huddled around nineteen-year-old Benji Cohn as he lay in a coma in an Orlando hospital emergency room at dawn.

Earlier that Saturday morning, at a teen night club, he had experimented with something that supposedly would give him a high sensation. Benji had sprayed horse tranquilizer on his tongue, then swallowed. In moments he had passed out, and someone called an ambulance.

His parents, Bob and Judy, prayed most of the fifty miles they traveled to get to the hospital. Pulling into the parking lot, Bob took Judy's hand. "We can't go into that hospital with any unbelief. You and I have to agree that no matter what the doctors tell us, we will believe God for Benji's total healing."

Judy agreed. Then she prayed something she would later remember well: "Lord, we choose to believe for Benji's total restoration in body, soul, and spirit."

Doctors were pessimistic, to say the least. "We do not know anything else to do," they told the Cohns. "We have done what the poison control has advised. It's a wait and see situation. If he comes out of this coma, he may be brain damaged. We have no idea how much time elapsed when oxygen wasn't getting to his brain," they added.

Judy and Bob stayed by their son for the next three hours, praying nonstop and talking to him as though he understood. "We love you and Jesus loves you," they reassured him.

The doctors thumped Benji's feet and chest to try to get a response. But his body did not respond to stimuli. He remained in a coma.

Judy suddenly felt something rise up within her—boldness, aggressiveness. She wasn't sure what, but she heard herself say in a very loud voice: "In Jesus' name, you wake up, Benji. Now! You will not leave us!"

Suddenly Benji bolted straight up in bed, choking. Doctors standing nearby were astonished. For the remainder of the day Benji drifted in and out of deep sleep. Moved into intensive care, he stayed on the respirator until five o'clock that evening.

When his parents left briefly, a nurse assigned to Benji came into his room. He remembers her saying, "This is a spiritual war, son. God's angels and the demons are fighting for you." Evidently she saw something in his room that he didn't.

When his parents returned, Benji asked them to forgive him. Then he asked God to forgive him. His prayer ended with, "Now, Jesus, come into my spirit and change me."

Judy remembered her prayer, that God would heal Benji in body, soul, and spirit. When he left the hospital on Monday, he was, in fact, healed in all three areas. His doctors were amazed. The Cohns knew God had answered their prayers, especially when Judy had commanded Benji to wake up in Jesus' name.

When Judy got home, she talked to a woman intercessor from her church who knew no details about Benji except that he had been in a coma. That Saturday she had asked God how to pray for Benji. As she prayed, she saw the scenario described by the hospital nurse: demons fighting the angels for Benji's life, even trying to suffocate him. She then knew how to pray more effectively. That weekend she joined her prayers with dozens of others from the Cohns' church.

Amazingly, Benji suffered no side effects for his ordeal—not even a sore throat from all the tubes that were inserted.

Perhaps Benji's story—and others in this section—help you recall some critical occasion in your life when you were miraculously saved from death or spared from calamity. Perhaps it was an escape from a fire, a near plane crash, a car accident. Perhaps you didn't see angels, but you know that only their presence can explain the unexplainable. Protection is just one role of God's angels. A Scripture search will further show you specific things that angels do and how they work. I have listed a few to help you get started.

Praying the Scriptures
GOD'S ANGELS WILL GUARD YOU

The angel of the LORD *encamps around those who fear him, and he delivers them.*

PSALM 34:7

See that you do not look down on one of these little ones. For I tell you that their angels in heaven always see the face of my Father in heaven.

MATTHEW 18:10

Are not all angels ministering spirits sent to serve those who will inherit salvation?

HEBREWS 1:14

If you make the Most High your dwelling—even the LORD, *who is my refuge—then no harm will befall you, no disaster will come near your tent. For he will command his angels concerning you to guard you in all your ways; they will lift you up in their hands, so that you will not strike your foot against a stone.*

PSALM 91: 9–12

In the same way, I tell you, there is rejoicing in the presence of the angels of God over one sinner who repents.

LUKE 15:10

When the Son of Man comes in his glory, and all the angels with him, he will sit on his throne in heavenly glory.

MATTHEW 25:31

Then Peter came to himself and said, "Now I know without a doubt that the Lord sent his angel and rescued me from Herod's clutches. . . ."

ACTS 12:11

PART SIX

Miracles of Healing

Praise the LORD, O my soul, and forget not all his benefits—who forgives all your sins and heals all your diseases, who redeems your life from the pit and crowns you with love and compassion.

PSALM 103:2–4

The good Instructor, the Wisdom, the Word of the Father, who made man, cares for the whole nature of his creature. The all-sufficient Physician of humanity, the Savior, heals both our body and soul, which are the proper man.

CLEMENT OF ALEXANDRIA

The same God who created our bodies has the power to heal them. And he is still healing today.

Many of us have been taught that miraculous healing ceased after the apostles died. Whenever we heard of someone getting healed by other than medical means, we wondered if it could be true. I was once in that category. I was raised in a church that did not emphasize healing, miracles, or prayer. But it was a healing miracle—resulting from prayer—that got my attention, changing my way of thinking and my prayer life forever.

While on vacation in 1972, I had gone with my Mom to a home meeting where people from her church were praying for Bill Lance, a young military veterinarian dying of acute leukemia. I was honest with God. Silently I told him, "Listen to their prayers, but count me out, Lord." I was a skeptic but open to whatever the Lord wanted to teach me. I continued my prayer, "I don't know if you still heal today, but I am willing to learn." The church had set aside a special "healing service" night for Bill before he entered the hospital, and the pastor and congregation believed he would be totally healed, I was told.

Though now chemotherapy was wreaking havoc with his body, causing hemorrhaging, pain, and anemia, it was not reducing the cancer. Doctors did not expect Bill to live through the weekend. Late that Friday night, in Bill's hospital room, he and his wife touched hands and repeated the Lord's Prayer, as was their usual pattern.

But this night tears suddenly cascaded down Bill's cheeks—hot tears that stung. Sobs convulsed him. He felt fire, like a charge of light, shooting through his body. The presence of Jesus filled the room. Bill couldn't explain what had just happened, even to Sharon.

The next morning doctors examined a bone marrow sample from his chest. It was normal—no sign of cancerous cells. Bill knew the hot light penetrating his body the night before was God's healing touch, flooding him through and through.

"Doctors say that leukemia is never healed, only that patients sometimes have a remission," he explained. "I was told the form I had rarely goes into remission. But I believe that Jesus Christ is the Great Physician." Nearly twenty-five years later, Bill is still healthy and active, and doctors have declared him totally healed.

Whenever I am prone to question God's healing power today, I remember Bill Lance and know I can continue to pray in faith that God will raise up the sick.[1]

Bill's story—and the others later in this section—remind me that it's my business to pray and God's business to heal. God heals by many means: the prayer of faith, medical aid, natural recuperative powers, and, yes, miracles—sometimes instantly, sometimes progressively.

Advocates of persistent prayer—some call it "soaking prayer"—suggest it may sometimes take time for healing to occur. This type of intercessory prayer is usually offered at regular intervals. A parent, for example, may pray for five minutes a day for her mentally handicapped child, or a group may gather once a week for thirty minutes to pray for a friend in a coma.

When pastor Dutch Sheets's wife, Ceci, had an ovarian cyst, he knew he needed to pray with perseverance and faith. The two of them asked the doctor to delay surgery for a while, so that Dutch could pray through the situation. For one hour every day for an entire month, he prayed specifically for his wife's cyst to dissolve. Throughout this time her pain continued to decrease. Then one day Dutch sensed that the work was finished and that he could quit praying for her healing. An ultrasound confirmed what he had sensed: The egg-sized cyst was gone![2]

This story and others show the value of one person praying for the healing of another. James 5:14–16 gives instruction about praying for others in the church:

Is any one of you sick? He should call the elders of the
church to pray over him and anoint him with oil in the
name of the Lord. And the prayer offered in faith will
make the sick person well; the Lord will raise him up.
If he has sinned, he will be forgiven. Therefore confess your sins to each other and pray for each other
so that you may be healed. The prayer of a righteous
man is powerful and effective.

In one gospel account Jesus healed a paralytic on the
faith of four friends who lowered him into Jesus' presence—
through the roof of the house. They were sure that their
friend would be healed if they could just get him to Jesus.
Jesus forgave the man's sins and then told him, "I tell you,
get up, take your mat and go home" (Mark 2:11). The man
walked out and everyone praised God.

Miracles are sometimes signs to those who do not yet
believe. We see this in the Acts of the Apostles, where Peter,
in the town of Lydda, met Aenaes, who had been paralyzed
and bedridden eight years. "'Aenaes,' Peter said to him,
'Jesus Christ heals you. Get up and take care of your mat.'
Immediately Aeneas got up. All those who lived in Lydda
and Sharon saw him and turned to the Lord" (Acts 9:33–
35). Notice that from this one miracle people from two com-
munities turned to God.

While God is still healing today, there is, of course,
no guarantee that every prayer for healing will result in a
miracle. The point is that we put our faith in God, not in
a miracle.

How should we pray? Let's begin by surrendering our
fear and anxiety to Christ. I call these the "what ifs." What
if I pray and I don't get well? What if I don't have enough
faith? Releasing all our "what ifs" (anxiety, worry, distrac-
tions, unbelief) into God's hands means trusting him, and
trust changes our whole perspective. Jesus instructed us not
to be anxious, for we are under the watchful care of our
heavenly Father (Matthew 6:25–34).

As I see it, faith and fear start out with the same definitions, in that both faith and fear believe something is going to happen. Fear believes something *bad* will happen, while faith believes something *good* will transpire. As I choose to trust God, I put my faith in God's promises or word to me.

Sometimes we start praying in one direction—out of our own fear—but as we pray, the Holy Spirit changes our prayer. We need to line up our will with God's and request God's presence, power, and guidance as we pray for the sick.

A SACRAMENTAL HEALING

Peggy Davis has lived all her life in the fishing village of Destin, Florida. She connects her quick, unexplained healing to Christ's healing power provided through the reception of Holy Communion or the Eucharist. Here is her account.[3]

As the winter sun was about to disappear over the Gulf of Mexico, I took advantage of the last touch of daylight to transfer some clothes from my sister's car into ours. I was about to slam the back door of our car when I looked up to see the headlights of a black beach buggy barreling right toward me. One moment it was a blur of light; the next, a crush of metal.

The impact swooped me onto the top of the car hood, and my head banged against the windshield. Then I was thrown from the vehicle, propelled through the air and spinning like a baseball that has been whacked mercilessly over center field. I remember praying, "Lord, do something. I can't stand this pain."

I landed on an asphalt road, and the pain increased. When my husband and sister got to me, they thought I was dead. I heard someone in the gathering crowd say my left leg was bleeding a lot.

In those moments, waiting for an ambulance, I felt especially close to Jesus.

A woman who had seen the accident bent down over me and asked what she could do. "Start praying," I pleaded. She placed a hand on my shoulder and prayed for my recovery.

An inner voice urged me to "hush and listen." About that time I heard my sister's little boy, Jamie, say, "Don't cry, Mama. Aunt Peggy's going to be all right."

Silently I affirmed, *Jesus is with me and I will be okay.*

The pain began to ease and a deep peace settled over me. I was in good hands—God's hands. Though my leg was still bleeding badly, all pain had left.

In the ambulance my husband and I recited the Lord's Prayer together. When we got to the hospital, doctors started working. It took more than one hundred stitches to close the gap in my left leg; the artery had been severed in two places. While the doctor stitched, my pastor, Forrest Mobley, held my hand and prayed for me. The peace I had felt earlier intensified. I later learned that an intercessory prayer group from our church, St. Andrews (Episcopal) by the Sea, had huddled for hours at the hospital, praying for me.

The medical tests indicated that I had a skull fracture and internal bleeding, and my doctor told me he intended to operate the next day.

Before surgery, my pastor returned, to give me Holy Communion. As he did, I heard the familiar prayer we repeat on Sundays, beseeching our merciful Father "to grant that, by the merits and death of thy Son Jesus Christ, and through faith in his blood, we, and all thy whole Church, may obtain remission of our sins, and all other benefits of his passion."

I cannot explain what happened next, but something mystical and supernatural occurred as I took the bread. The priest continued reading from the Book of Common Prayer: "The Body of our Lord Jesus Christ, which was given for thee, preserve thy body and soul unto everlasting life. Take and eat this in remembrance that Christ died for thee and feed on him in thy heart by faith, with thanksgiving."

As I swallowed the wine, he continued reading. "The Blood of our Lord Jesus Christ, which was shed for thee, preserve thy body and soul unto everlasting life. Drink this in remembrance that Christ's Blood was shed for thee and be thankful."

As I lay on that hospital bed, my Lord reached down and touched me with his healing power. The power of his Holy Spirit was wrapped around me. I knew I was healed.

The doctor came in and reevaluated my tests. He ordered new X-rays. I wasn't surprised when he later walked into my room with good news. "I came to the hospital this morning prepared to operate on you. But now we won't have to," he said.

The internal bleeding had stopped. I believe that when I took the elements of Holy Communion, the healing process began. Even the skull fracture failed to show up on new X-rays.

For the next few days everyone who came into my hospital room looked like shining jewels. I loved Jesus Christ as I never had before. His love reached out through me to everyone I saw.

I was in the hospital only five days. The next Sunday I was able to walk down the aisle of the church on crutches to receive Holy Communion at the altar rail. Tears spilled down my face as I praised God for my healing. I praised him, too, for all the people he had sent into my life to pray for and encourage me.

It has been more than twenty years since a black beach buggy swooped me up and sent me spinning onto an asphalt road. In the intervening years God has helped me to live more effectively for him.

As she took Communion in the hospital, Peggy experienced a totally new realization of Christ's body broken for her, his blood shed for her sins, and his stripes as her healing portion. Who can understand how one can be healed during Eucharist—a word meaning "giving of thanks"? Celebrated from the first days of the church, the bread and cup symbolize the body and blood of Christ, remembering his sacrificial death. As we prepare ourselves today to take Communion, we must engage in self-examination, penitence of heart, and faith to get our hearts ready to receive the elements.

Peggy's healing is but one of many I have heard about that occurred as a person received Communion. It is one of God's mysteries. And we are the grateful recipients—giving thanks for his healing goodness.

ONE HEALING LEADS TO ANOTHER

Peggy's healing led to another healing, and to still another—like a row of dominos. Peggy's cousin Ben Marler, Jr., was touched by the story of her healing. He especially remembered Peggy saying how she had felt at the accident scene—that Jesus was with her and that she would be okay. Ben tells his story:

After Peggy was struck by the car, I was surprised she was able to walk. She had looked like an Egyptian mummy with all the bandages tightly wrapped about her body. I had heard her tell her healing story several times, so I guess I had almost memorized it.

A few weeks later, while on a deer hunting expedition on St. Vincent Island off Apalachicola, I was sitting about eight feet above the ground on a large tree limb—which snapped. When I landed, my left leg was caught under me, my knee dislocated.

Screaming in pain, I pushed into the ground with my right boot and pulled on a sapling with my hand. The effort allowed my body to slide off of my leg. The knee "popped" back into place resulting in even greater pain, somewhat like fire shooting through it. I cried out, "Dear Jesus, help me." Suddenly I heard a vehicle slowly approaching. When it was close, I whistled as loud as I could, and I was picked up by a federal biologist who heard my distress call. "Something told me to drive down this old washboard road on my way to get gas today," he said.

The ride in the truck was excruciating, every little bump causing the pain to crescendo. We would travel about fifty feet when I would scream for the driver to stop the truck. After going a short distance, with many stops, I remembered Peggy's injury. I started telling her story to my driver, and when I reached the place where Peggy had said, "Jesus is with me and I will be okay," something miraculous happened to me. The pain in my knee vanished!

I wept unashamedly as I told the driver that God had just touched my knee. It was the first time I knew for sure he really loved me, even though I had sung "Jesus Loves Me, This I Know" hundreds of times.

Arriving back home in Destin in my Bronco, I called my pastor. He came to my home and anointed my knee with oil. The next day, my doctor X-rayed it and told me to go home and use it. It was sore, but the discomfort was mild compared to the first pangs. I had been granted a miracle.

Later while teaching customers to catch fish on my deep sea charter boat, *Her Majesty II*, I shared with them the story of my knee being healed at the moment when I had said aloud, "Jesus is with me and I will be okay." One of my regular customers from Montgomery was listening intently as I spoke. I noticed a sudden change in her face. I did not know she had just reached under the table and touched her bad knee—a knee that often gave way under her.

This woman told me later that from that moment on she never had any further trouble with it. She fished with me for several years afterwards. Each time I inquired about her knee she would report, "It's fine. No more trouble. None since that day it was healed on your boat."

When we realize God loves us enough to perform a miracle in answer to our prayer, faith takes on a deeper dimension. We experience his compassion and power in a fresh new way. That's what happened to Ben and to his charter-boat customer, both of whom received a healing touch from God.

WHEN NO ONE ELSE BELIEVED

As soon as the doctor came into her hospital room, Sandy Horn planned to shake her fists in his face and demand that he tell her the truth about the extent of her malignancy.

The doctor and Sandy's husband, Earl, were huddling out in the hall, deciding how much to tell her. They decided to lay out the facts. When they entered the room, the doctor took the X-rays he had brought and pointed to five malignant spots he had circled. She had cancer in her neck, in the top and bottom left ribs, in her pelvic bone, and at the tip of her spine. When his only prescription was cobalt treatment, the seriousness of his words hit her. She had inoperable cancer.

Sandy was thirty-four-years old, bursting with enthusiasm for life and enjoying the gypsy style of moving wherever the space industry transferred Earl. They had three healthy young children, who needed her. She desperately fought the thought of dying so young. She tells her story:[4]

God was my only hope. I was used to taking my problems to him, and I turned to him now with specific prayers for healing. I felt so close to him as I whiled away those lonely afternoons in bed, searching the Scriptures for promises I knew he would reveal.

When I was thirteen, soon after my baptism in a Tennessee mountain stream, I had heard a preacher say that God still heals sick bodies. But my aunt had convinced me that miracles were outdated. Now as I lay on my sick bed afternoon after afternoon, I could not find anything in my Bible telling me miracles were exclusively for first-century Christians.

I began to claim the promise of healing, especially as I read and reread from my old King James Bible the Scripture from James 5:14 that says to call the elders of the church to pray over the sick, anointing them with oil in the name of the Lord, and the prayer of faith would save the sick person. I asked God to send me some elders. I didn't think the elders in my own church would consider such a prayer, but I knew somehow God would work it out. I believed I would be healed even when no one else wanted to talk about it. My husband, Earl, was especially annoyed when I brought up the subject.

Over the next few weeks I underwent thirty-four cobalt treatments—but only in the throat area, where the first cancer had shown up. Doctors would later decide which malignant spot would be treated next. After all, I had five.

I had to make the one-hundred-and-thirty mile round trip from my home to the hospital each day. As the weeks stretched out, I realized the importance of *time.* How I treasured it—time with my family, time spent talking to God.

Some days I had a real battle with self-pity. "It isn't fair," I would wail. "I'm five hundred miles from my mother, and there's nobody to help care for me." Earl had to leave early for his job, so each morning, no matter how I felt, I got Donna and Ricky off to school and took Jim in the car with me—for a sixty-five mile drive into Hattiesburg, Mississippi.

As the cobalt treatments in my throat progressed, various muscles began to collapse. The doctor said the inside of my throat was starting to look like a raw piece of beef. Yet despite everything, I believed Jesus would heal me.

In the meantime each night I prayed for strength to make it through the next day. "Just enough, Lord, to make it to the hospital and home again," I would ask.

As I grew weaker, little Jim and I sang Christmas carols so I wouldn't fall asleep while driving. Soon I was depending on my three-year-old son to zip my dress. Eventually friends volunteered to drive me to the hospital each day. How I needed them!

Late one Sunday night, right before Christmas, my pastor and a visiting Taiwanese missionary knocked on our door. Could they pray for me? they asked. Surely they were the elders I had prayed would come!

They prayed specifically that God would heal me. After they left, I stretched out in bed beside Earl. As I began praising God silently, a strange sensation pulsated through my body, much like an ocean wave engulfing me.

I felt a surge of power wash up from my toes, extend to my head, and rush back down through my body to my toes again. The power of Jesus had healed my body! I had met my risen Lord as I had never met him before.

I nudged my sleeping husband. "I am healed, Earl. I am healed," I said excitedly.

"I'm glad," he mumbled as he fell back into a deep sleep, obviously not taking me seriously.

I sank to my knees beside the bed, praising God and thanking him for healing me.

In the weeks that followed I shared my belief in my healing with my friends. "I'm healed," I repeated over and over again.

"That's nice, but don't get your hopes up."

"Jesus healed me," I would tell someone else.

"It's not good for you to get excited," they would answer.

"Earl, I know that Jesus came to me and healed me."

"Sandy, I don't think that kind of talk is too good for you right now."

I waited impatiently for the first week of February, when I was scheduled to go into the hospital for scans to see where they should start the next cobalt treatment. Supposedly the scans would determine where the malignancy was spreading the fastest. I knew the scan would show I'd been healed.

The day before I was to check into the hospital, I was suddenly frightened. What if everybody else was right and I was wrong? What if God hadn't really healed me and I had only imagined the physical sensation?

That afternoon my daughter came home from a friend's house, carrying a copy of *Guideposts*. In it I read a story of former Army General Bruce Medaris, onetime head of Redstone Arsenal, where my husband worked. The magazine told how he had been divinely healed of cancer. "Of course God is still healing today," I shouted, "and he has healed me too."

I woke the next morning to the tune of soft choir music. I heard each word clearly as voices blended singing about Jesus, my friend. Jumping out of bed I found an old church song book. There I found the words to the song I had just heard, though it had been twenty years since I had last sung it: "There's not a friend like the lowly Jesus—No, not one! No, not one!" Had I heard a heavenly choir? My assurance returned. I had a deep feeling there would be no need for further cobalt treatments.

After one day of scans and another day of X-rays, the radiologist gave me the results. "You have won the first round," he said. "Nothing showed up." They ran more tests. Again, no sign of cancer.

Earl and I asked to see both sets of scans—the original ones showing the five malignant spots and the scans just completed. Looking at them, we knew I was home free. Well! Complete! Whole! Healed! "Thank God!" I cried tears of happiness and joy. Earl rushed to telephone our closest friends, not afraid now to tell them, "Sandy's been healed by Jesus."

As I began my last trip home from the hospital, a Bible verse kept running through my mind. "Return home and tell how much God has done for you" (Luke 8:39a).

That was twenty-eight years ago. Earl became a Christian as a result of my healing, and I have had many opportunities to tell others that the supernatural power of God is available for healing today.

Sandy, who had faith when others doubted, continues to tell anyone who will listen that healing is still available for Christians who will ask for it, believing. She says she is, after all, living proof of a healing miracle.

WOULD GOD REALLY HEAL HER?

Sande Lofberg believed God could heal, but would he? As Lord of the universe, did he not have more important issues to attend to than touching her body? She thought so. I will let Sande tell you about her miracle.

In the late 1950s I developed asthma. I was also allergic to many animals, plants, and foods. I controlled my symptoms with a combination of shots and oral and inhaled medications. Several times I had to be hospitalized for breathing difficulties. On other occasions my husband had to take me to the emergency room for treatment.

My husband's Air Force career took us to England, where the damp cold and the air pollution caused my condition to worsen. When we returned to Idaho, the air was drier, but pollen and dust became a major problem.

I began attending a Bible study taught by a chaplain's wife. One week she read selections from a book about ordinary people who had been healed of all kind of afflictions. I had already taken my medicines that morning. Even so, as she read, I began to wheeze. The wheezing increased and was painful because I also had a case of pleurisy, an inflammation of the lining of the lung. Nancy, the study leader, came to sit next to me. "Do you believe Jesus can heal you?" she asked.

Just a few weeks earlier I had acknowledged Jesus as my Savior. I believed he *could* heal. But I didn't think he *would*. Why, there were many more problems in the world larger than my need! But I answered yes to Nancy's question. She prayed, asking Jesus to touch my body and heal me.

In moments, a warm sensation filled my body, radiating from my chest. I stopped wheezing. I coughed several times and took a deep breath. Then another breath, deeper than I could ever remember taking. In my joy, I stretched both hands up over my head, without any pain.

I knew Jesus had died for the sins of the world, but this physical healing was something very personal. He wasn't "too busy" to show his love and power to a woman who had just begun to know him.

That was in 1975. I have been free of asthma and allergies ever since, even after returning to England for two more tours of duty with my husband.

Sande received a healing touch from God—even when she was hesitant to believe. Maybe you too think God is too busy for your problem. He's not. Just turn to him and talk to him about your greatest need.

HEALED OVERNIGHT

When Nick Lovitt was twenty-five, he broke a bone in his left foot as he tripped over a grocery cart. It quickly developed into painful rheumatoid arthritis. If you saw the successful Colorado real estate broker today, you would have no clue how crippled he once was.

He shares his story:

Within forty-eight hours after I broke my left foot, gout set in. Over the next two years as it progressed, three different doctors diagnosed my condition as "gouty rheumatoid arthritis." The joints swelled in my left leg—foot, toes, ankle, knee, and hip. Calcium spurs developed on the bottom of both feet and in my left ankle and knee.

I was taking three of the most powerful pain drugs available. In addition, I swallowed thirty to forty aspirin a day, but the medication did not suppress all my intense pain.

When I stood for the first time each morning, the torturing pain felt like nails being driven into the bottoms of my feet. The big toe on my left foot swelled to two inches in diameter and the left ankle to fourteen inches in circumference, twice its normal size. I couldn't walk without a cane.

My ability to function in real estate was greatly impaired. I would drive my customers to a house and let them walk through to see it themselves to save myself the pain of standing. After two-and-one-half years of this—even while taking in excess of eighty pills a day—I knew I could not endure the pain much longer.

On a November night in 1971, I was desperate. "Lord, I cannot go on with this pain and be a good father, husband, and provider for my family. The pain is too much for me. I can't take it anymore. Lord Jesus, you must heal me or take me home. Please do something," I continued, sobbing like a baby.

I went to the medicine cabinet. As my wife watched in amazement, I flushed down the commode fourteen different bottles of pills plus two thousand aspirin. I was still sobbing and crying aloud. Then I went to bed not knowing what was going to happen.

The next morning I awoke on my back—a big switch after sleeping on my stomach for more than two years to avoid more intense pain. Something dramatic had happened in my body. I put my feet over the side of the bed and stood up immediately. No pain! No pain! No pain!

Cautiously, I walked out onto the tile floor. Then I ran outside, up and down the concrete sidewalk. Still no pain! I was crying, knowing I had been completely healed of gouty arthritis.

That very day I went back to the doctor and asked him to X-ray my feet. He compared them to previous X-rays, taken just two weeks before. He was astounded. Every calcium spur was gone. He had only one plausible explanation: Had I passed kidney stones—itself an excruciating ordeal?

"No," I told him pointedly, "I asked God to heal me."

"Medically, it is impossible for this to happen," he responded, still studying the two sets of X-rays. But God had performed my miracle instantly. In the twenty-five years since, I have not had a sign of reoccurrence.

The Miracle-Worker is still at work—on duty night and day.

THE POWER OF A DYING MAN'S PRAYER

Mark Ewing had just turned thirty that winter of 1981, and he could not throw off his fatigue. He was rapidly losing weight, and the doctors were unable to tell him why.

Finally, chest X-rays and a biopsy on the lymph nodes revealed the awful truth: Hodgkins disease—cancer of the lymphatic system. Mark's father had been a physician and his mother a nurse, and though they were retired, they had never heard of anyone who had survived Hodgkins.

To determine how far the cancer had progressed, he traveled north from Florida to Emory University Hospital in

Atlanta. After numerous probings, Mark was diagnosed as having seriously advanced cancer, which had gone undiagnosed six months or more. He also had an inoperable chest tumor.

He was terribly emaciated, his body seeming to waste away; he was down to 125 pounds and coughed constantly. Finally, he was wheeled to surgery to remove his spleen and, through the use of other biopsies, to determine the extent of his diseases.

Tests showed that chemotherapy was a possibility. But, Mark wondered, would it really help? "God, I so want to live," he prayed one afternoon, looking out at the blooming dogwood outside his hospital room.

A young Georgia lawyer named Tom, who had bone cancer, was in a room down the hall from Mark. Tom's family and Mark's parents and wife became acquainted and prayed together for both young men. One day Mark asked to be wheeled down to meet Tom, who was in excruciating pain; he would rock himself back and forth on his hands and knees in his hospital bed. The motion seemed to ease him or take his mind off the pain.

Tom told Mark, "I can't sleep at night, so I'll take it as my time to pray for you to be healed." Nights seemed the darkest for Mark as well—when he hurt most, coughed more, and had to fight the hardest to live.

Sometimes Mark also prayed for Tom. It had touched him deeply that Tom, a man much closer to death than he was, would pledge to pray for him, a virtual stranger. Somehow this comforted him.

Mark soon returned home, to receive chemotherapy on familiar territory. He and his wife, Karen, moved in with his parents. Life and death questions hung in the air. Even if the drugs worked against the cancer, would he be able to enjoy life to the fullest? Would he, for instance, be able to father children?

Pale and shaky, Mark went to church with his parents on the first Sunday he was strong enough. That day the entire congregation prayed for Mark's healing. After church, a woman whom he did not know gave him a scribbled note, saying in essence that God was going to heal him. "From that encouragement I knew I wasn't going to die of Hodgkins," says Mark. "Whenever I'd feel awful, I would fall back on that word."

Over a six-month period he received twelve powerful treatments, each of which caused extreme nausea. But Mark began to gain weight, and every check-up gave more hope.

Mark held on to a scriptural promise: "Though you have made me see troubles, many and bitter, you will restore my life again; from the depths of the earth you will again bring me up. You will increase my honor and comfort me once again" (Psalm 71:20–21). And so God did. He restored Mark's life and comforted him through his ordeal of treatment.

It has been fifteen years since Mark's initial bout with cancer. He was not only healed, but he has also fathered two healthy sons and works as administrative dean of students at a high school.

It may be true that Mark received his healing miracle from a combination of medical help and prayer. But Mark knows he received a healing grace from God. "A lot of things in my life have changed since then," he says. "I have especially grown a lot closer to the Lord."

Some weeks after Mark got back to Florida, Tom's wife called to say he had died two weeks after Mark's discharge. His last breaths, she said, were spent praying for Mark. Mark was moved to tears. He thanked God for such devotion and for all those prayers!

Why do some people die and others live? Questions such as this will never be answered this side of heaven. Our part is to pray for healing, and God's part is to do the rest. In this instance, the faith of a dying, selfless man figured in the answer of God's plan for another young man named Mark.

Our Lord may give you the grace to endure suffering, or he may give you the grace to be healed. Whatever happens, your life is in his hands and he is making something beautiful out of it.

Praying the Scriptures
EMBRACE GOD AS HEALER

God still performs healing miracles. I know; I have been privileged to write many miraculous healing stories for magazines and books since that night long ago when I told God I wasn't sure he healed. Believers sitting around me prayed for Bill Lance to be healed of leukemia, and God touched him powerfully. If you are needing such a healing, don't give up! Miracles are still part of God's provision.

I have heard your prayer and seen your tears; I will heal you.

2 KINGS 20:5

O LORD my God, I called to you for help and you healed me.

PSALM 30:2

Jesus went throughout Galilee . . . healing every disease and sickness among the people.

MATTHEW 4:23

He sent forth his word and healed them; he rescued them from the grave.

PSALM 107:20

Heal me, O LORD, and I will be healed; save me and I will be saved, for you are the one I praise.

JEREMIAH 17:14

I have been crucified with Christ and I no longer live, but Christ lives in me. The life I live in the body, I live by faith in the Son of God, who loved me and gave himself for me.

GALATIANS 2:20

He himself bore our sins in his body on the tree, so that we might die to sins and live for righteousness; by his wounds you have been healed.

1 PETER 2:24

And these signs will accompany those who believe: In my name they will . . . place their hands on sick people, and they will get well.

MARK 16:17–18

Dear friend, I pray that you may enjoy good health and that all may go well with you, even as your soul is getting along well.

3 JOHN 2

PART SEVEN

Miracles of Protection

*For in the day of trouble he will keep me safe
in his dwelling; he will hide me in the shelter
of his tabernacle and set me high upon a rock.*
PSALM 27:5

I have found the perfect antidote for fear. Whenever it sticks up its ugly face I clobber it with prayer.

DALE EVANS ROGERS

*T*hroughout the Bible, God has revealed himself as a fortress, a refuge, a source of strength, a stronghold in time of trouble, and the defender of widows and orphans. This is the same God who hears our prayers and sometimes answers them with a miracle.

The startling truth is that God himself watches over us every moment of the day and night. As Jesus reminds us: "Are not two sparrows sold for a penny? Yet not one of them will fall to the ground apart from the will of your Father. And even the very hairs of your head are all numbered. So don't be afraid; you are worth more than many sparrows" (Matthew 10:29–31).

Ultimately, it is God himself we must rely on as our Protector—when confronted with crisis, natural disaster, sickness, physical infirmity, political upheaval, or whatever calamity we face. Have you ever read some of the "miraculous escapes" in the Bible and marveled at how they relied on God's protection? I have. One of my favorite accounts is in 2 Chronicles 20, a marvelous miracle of protection with three parts: the king's prayer, the Lord's response, and the great victory.

In Jerusalem King Jehoshaphat received a report that a great multitude "from the other side of the Sea" was coming to wage war against him and his people. Afraid, he turned to God for direction and protection. He began by proclaiming a fast throughout all Judah, during which the people humbled themselves before the Lord. Fasting is an outward indication of humility and the urgency that is felt when praying for a specific need.

The people's first step to victory was prayer that accompanied the fasting. Jehoshaphat stood before the assembled people and recalled God's past blessings in a powerful prayer, reminding the Lord that they were under Abraham's covenant (God's promises). He admitted his helplessness as he prayed: "If calamity comes upon us, whether the sword of judgment, or plague or famine, we will stand in your presence before this temple that bears your Name and will cry out to you in our distress, and you will hear us and save us" (verse 9).

The king declared his utter dependence on God. He then reminded God that he had given them their land and that the enemy intended to take their inheritance away from them. His prayer for help, in summary, said (verse 12):

- We have no strength or power on our own;
- we do not know what to do;
- but our eyes are on God.

All the families stood before the Lord that day. The Spirit of the Lord then came upon a man named Jahaziel, who delivered a prophecy (verses 15–17):

"This is what the LORD says to you:
- Do not be afraid or discouraged. . . .
- The battle is not yours, but God's. . . .
- Take your positions;
- stand firm
- and see the deliverance the LORD will give you. . . .
- Go out to face them tomorrow, and the LORD will be with you."

Jehoshaphat and the people then fell down to worship the Lord.

As instructed, the next morning the people set out for battle. As they marched, the king appointed men to sing to the Lord, the singers leading the army. As they sang praises, God sent ambushes against the enemy armies, and they fought each other. When Jehoshaphat's army arrived, they found only dead bodies. It took them three days to collect the spoils. On the fourth day, they gathered to praise the Lord. They had not even had to fight, but they had followed God's instruction, stood firm, and watched him bring deliverance.

As you expect miracles from God, I suggest you pray, expect a word from him (maybe even explicit instructions), praise him, and stand firm with trust.

How can we pray for protection? Here are some practical ways:

- Ask God to keep us alert to danger, so we will not make foolish mistakes or unwise choices.
- Ask God to keep his angels about us to guard us in all our ways.
- Ask God for supernatural strength and wisdom when we need it most.
- When we find ourselves in a dangerous situation, ask God for the best way out, for his direction.
- Ask God for his peace in times when we want to panic and run.
- Learn faith-building Scriptures to use in a crisis, so that fear will not consume us.
- Pray for one another daily.

So many today live in fear—for ourselves, for our children, and for the next generation. In the midst of our challenges and fears, God is still sovereign. Society's character might change, but God's character never does. God really is in control even in a chaotic world. Jesus, in teaching the Lord's Prayer, told us to pray "Deliver us from evil." Our prayers can make a difference in our protection.

HER DELIVERER IN TROUBLED WATERS

Paula Shields needed God as her Deliverer in her troubled waters. Her very life depended upon him. She tells us her story:

I had gone whitewater rafting before and made plans to go again. Verna, my coadventurer, picked the Kern River near Bakersfield, California. When we met in California, we visited friends of hers. One of them, a nurse, told us several had already died on that river that summer. She begged us not to go out; the river was running very high. High, of course, means more power and more water, but also more danger. We laughed as we told her we were going with an experienced guide, so not to worry.

The next day at breakfast in a restaurant, we told our waitress what we were doing. She too warned us. "People have lost their lives rafting in that river." Again we laughed.

As we left the restaurant, a man walked over to us and asked what we were doing. When we told him, he too cautioned us that we should not go on the river.

I do not know why we didn't heed the warnings. I know that once I make a decision, I want to follow through with it. And we did, though we made sure we got on the same raft as the head guide for our whole group. After we had maneuvered safely through two sets of rapids, we saw trouble. People on the raft ahead of us had flipped into the water. Our raft—with the head guide—had to lead the rescue. But as we did so, our raft flipped over—and in a very dangerous spot, near trees. Our guides had already alerted us that if anyone fell in the water near these trees, he or she could easily be "sucked down."

And I was! Though I had on a life jacket, I swirled down, down, down, out of control. I was underwater and unable to come up. I am usually very buoyant and can hardly stay under water. What was wrong? Then I realized my left leg was stuck in the tree roots underwater.

I could not move! *I'm going to die—to drown—unless something drastic happens.*

A Bible verse popped into my head: Call on the name of Jesus and you will be saved. I needed to be saved. So I mentally repeated the name of Jesus, over and over. *Jesus, Jesus, Jesus.*

As I did, my leg miraculously came free, and I shot up to the surface, where I still sensed danger. I was being pulled downstream by churning water, and out ahead I could hear the roar of the next rapids—fast approaching. I tried to grab hold of tree branches as I rushed by them. Three broke off in my hands. Finally, a fourth branch held me.

Climbing that branch, I pulled myself out of the current. Holding on for dear life, I turned around to check on the other rafters being rescued. As I waited to be picked up, hoping and praying my branch would hold, I contemplated what I should do. *Praise God in everything,* I thought. *But how do I praise God in this dire situation?* An old Fanny Crosby hymn came to my mind:

> Pass me not O gentle Savior—
> Hear my humble cry!
> While on others Thou art calling,
> Do not pass me by.

I started singing this aloud. Then I just praised God. Finally the raft with the rescuers worked their way toward me, and I was thrown a lifeline.

It takes great courage to let go of the safety of your branch to grab hold of a lifeline. But I did. They pulled me into the raft. I started shaking violently, because I was in shock. When I later tried to walk, I had a limp in my left leg, which had been trapped under that tree.

I learned much through my near brush with death in the turbulent waters. God had tried to warn me three times through people I didn't even know. I ignored the cautions because I wanted to go whitewater rafting, and I was determined to do it. I need to listen more. Now I try to check with him about everything I do, even fun time.

A year after the incident I heard about an amazing story of intercession on my behalf. At the very moment I was trapped under water, an acquaintance of mine in Holland was praying specifically for me. I came to her mind; she sensed I was in danger and interceded for my safety and protection. I believe her prayers were instrumental in my life being spared. I realize how important it is to respond to those little "nudges" we get from the Holy Spirit to pray. It can be a matter of life and death for someone.

How gratifying for Paula to discover someone was praying for her safety at the very moment she needed intercession. That is one key for protection. We pray for one another, especially if someone's name happens to suddenly come to mind. Or perhaps we have a roster of folks we pray for regularly—family and friends, perhaps. God will impress us with the names of those for whom he wants us to intercede. Be faithful to do so at the moment you feel alerted to pray.

The apostle Paul wrote the Colossians about a friend named Epaphras, who "is always wrestling in prayer for you, that you may stand firm in all the will of God, mature and fully assured" (Colossians 4:12). Wouldn't it be great if each of us had friends who would wrestle in prayer for us? We can be the intercessors who stand in the prayer gap for others too.

MISSING THE WALL

As I have mentioned, fasting and prayer often yield directions and answers from God, a new understanding of Scripture, a closer walk with God, a humbling of oneself, a healing, or even a deliverance.

Lynda Brooks believes her fast played a role in her deliverance or protection in a potentially deadly situation. She describes her experience.

Though I do not enjoy fasting, I felt I should undertake a three-day fast, consuming only water and juice, while spending some extra time in prayer. I wasn't sure why or what I was fasting for, just sensing the need to pray in this way.

It was around noon on my second day of fasting. I left downtown Nashville for my home in the suburbs, traveling by Interstate 65, the freeway.

For several weeks I had been "hearing" sounds of crashing metal and broken glass, the way you "hear" a catchy song that plays over and over in your mind. It was so odd that I had mentioned it to my husband. Why would I be hearing something that wasn't even real? Was the Holy Spirit warning me of something?

One Scripture I was meditating on during this time was: "He holds victory in store for the upright, he is a shield to those whose walk is blameless, for he guards the course of the just and protects the way of his faithful ones" (Proverbs 2:7–8).

As I drove home, traveling sixty-five miles per hour, I listened to a tape of a sermon on Psalm 91, the psalm of protection. I heard the minister say, "When trouble surrounds you, God will be with you and rescue you. . . ."

Then I suddenly heard the real crashing metal and broken glass. A thought flashed through my mind, *This is exactly what I've been hearing in my head for weeks.*

An eighteen wheeler had changed lanes, cutting in front of me and swatting my car with the power of a giant whale. The driver must not have seen me, for he never even stopped. My car bounced up and down, but not sideways, so it missed the nearby cement wall separating the highway lanes. A woman who saw the accident was as surprised as I was that my car didn't hit the wall.

The powerful impact totaled my car; yet I, who would have normally reacted with fear, felt only peace—God's peace. I have been in wrecks before, and I know how frightened I get. But not this time. I believe my lack of fear was related to my fasting and prayer. Maybe the sounds I had heard were warnings to prepare me.

During my time of prayer and fasting I had felt so close to the Lord. I know he rescued me, preventing my car from slamming against the wall. I thanked God for being my shield! Whenever he impresses me to fast, I am quick to do it.

NO SUCH THING AS A "LUCKY" MIRACLE

God helped Ed Hilton escape from his truck moments before it exploded in fire and flames devoured his truckload of paper. Ed had driven probably fifty thousand miles in Dallas traffic with no incidents until this hit-and-run accident. He tells his story:

How close I came to death! I could have been knocked unconscious or trapped in the cab to die that fateful spring afternoon, leaving my two beautiful children without a father and my wife a widow.

On March 19, 1996, about five o'clock in the afternoon, I was making a routine delivery for the courier company I worked for. In the back of my truck was ten thousand pounds of paper—six full skids of computer paper. I was traveling north on 75 Central in Dallas. The highway is four lanes wide, and I was in the second to right lane. The traffic was moderate.

All of a sudden I heard brakes squealing and saw a fast-moving car cutting across the lanes, hitting my truck and causing me to lose control. My vehicle rammed through a guard rail, taking down a steel lamp post as it went. Then I realized the truck was going off the side of some sort of bridge. I remember calling out, "Lord, help me!"

The truck rolled and landed upside down on an entrance ramp, about ten feet below, then slid several feet. The cab area was crushed, the windshield was blown out, and hot oil was pouring into the cab from the engine.

As soon as I shut off the ignition, I saw something was on fire. The next thing I knew—just seconds, it seemed— the truck burst into flames. "Jesus, please help me get out," I screamed. Managing to unbuckle my seat belt, I scrambled out through the smashed windshield.

The medical team at the hospital could not believe I was not seriously hurt. I had some cuts, singed hair, and a couple of minor burns. The doctor said I was lucky. But luck did not save me; God's hand of protection saved me.

After two hours of examinations and treatment, I was released.

Later when I saw the truck, I could not believe the wreckage; it was smashed almost flat.

Afterward this Scripture came to me: "When you walk through the fire, you will not be burned; the flames will not set you ablaze. For I am the LORD, your God, the Holy One of Israel, your Savior ..." (Isaiah 43:2b–3a).

I have thought a lot about how close I came to being killed, as certainly would have happened had I not gotten out of the truck before it exploded! If the seat belt had not unsnapped, if the windshield had not been smashed open.... I thank God that I'm alive, and I am determined to fulfill God's will for my life.

Some miracles are "escapes" and an opportunity to fulfill God's purpose with new meaning, determination, and thankfulness.

ESCAPE FROM FIRE

More than two thousand acres of nearby woods were burning. Could Ray Meyers's home on Choctawhatchee Bay in the Florida panhandle escape? Ray's was the first and only house under construction in a new thickly wooded subdivision.

That morning a contractor clearing debris to put in a road just three miles west of Ray's place piled brush and old stumps—and lit them. Soon the wind picked up, fanning flames into the woods. The volunteer fire department had no road access to the fire's origin. Flames and smoke moved toward the south and east.

As the smoke approached Ray's partially built house, his contractor's men stopped hammering, climbed into their pick-ups, and drove away. "This house is insured. Get out now; this fire is too big to stop," the carpenter foreman shouted at Ray as he made his getaway.

Fifteen minutes later a sheriff's deputy arrived. "Leave the area as soon as you can," he advised.

Ray's builder and a friend from his church lingered with Ray at the site. The three men knelt in the yard and prayed. "Lord, spare this house. You know it will be used for you. ..." Ray's wife, Carol, at their rented home some twenty miles away, paced up and down, earnestly praying for her husband's safety and their property's protection.

The three men finished praying. Though things didn't look good, Ray felt confident and peaceful. His friends left, and Ray got in his own car. But he didn't drive away.

Ray picks up his story:

I was last to leave, staring at the house in a half-finished condition. Was I going to come back to charred and smoking ruins? I drove toward the road entrance. No! I was not going to leave. I turned around and drove back to the house.

I took a hooded jacket from the car and pulled it on. Then I started walking around the house, picking up all the wood scraps so the fire would have less fuel. I threw them over the top of—into—the steel dumpster.

A small old fire engine pumper pulled up with two firemen on board. They were checking the area and didn't know there were any houses around. They begged me to leave. When they saw my determination to stay, they tried to wet down the house with their hoses, though that was a small effort against such a raging inferno.

I must have looked ridiculous standing with a garden hose in one hand, trying to stop a thirty foot wall of flames from engulfing the house. Suddenly the hose stopped squirting. No water. I looked down and realized it was on fire. I threw it down.

The wildfire was now about fifteen feet away. In only thirty seconds it had crossed the swamp three hundred feet from my house. It was roaring, consuming whole trees. The air was heavy with smoke. Coughing and gasping, I held my handkerchief over my mouth to help me breathe. Then I saw the steel dumpster with all the wood scraps shooting up in flames ten feet high.

I could feel the heat of the fire through my shirt and jacket. As I backed toward the house, flames were all around me. Then something spectacular happened. As fast as it had come, the fire shifted and moved away from my house. It was as though God had waved his hand, and the wind had changed course.

A ring of black, burned grass and woods surrounding our house gave evidence to the intensity and proximity of the fire. But it was over. I walked around to examine the house again. Black tinder had blown in through the window openings, but the house had no damage! As I walked back to where I had stood with the garden hose, I noticed the plastic flashing around the window frames had melted. I had stood between the fire and the plastic frames that had melted, and I was okay—still coughing, but okay!

The local television crew came out to film our house, unharmed, surrounded by a ring of black burned foliage. It was on the news the next night.

Word had gotten out that our house had been destroyed. But as we kept ordering building supplies to finish it, trucks making the deliveries all used the same unusual address: "Miracle House."

To this day, ten years later, there is a sign out front of Ray Meyers's large ranch-style home that reads "Miracle House." Bible studies have been conducted there steadily since its completion. What happened that day was remarkable. Some would say Ray's decision to stay at his house was a bit unwise. He wouldn't recommend that just anyone take his course of action. But he knows God heard his heart's cry and gave him a miracle. He has not stopped thanking God for the answer to his prayer.

A HIT AND RUN

In 1992 God's mercy in answering the prayers of hundreds from around the world played a role in Missy Lindsay's survival.[1] Those who saw her limp body sprawled in the road were sure she was dead.

Her dad is Dennis Lindsay, President of Christ for the Nations Institute in Dallas. The school was founded by his parents, Gordon and Freda Lindsay, whose early ministry and magazine were called *The Voice of Healing*. Miracles were the norm for their family.

Dennis Lindsay and his wife, Ginger, had just arrived in Cordoba, Argentina, for a week-long series of meetings for the students at the CFN campus there. But that first night he preached at a local church, where his topic was "God Cares for His Children." He emphasized how much our loving heavenly Father cares for his children. He spoke of God's invisible footprints; even though his presence isn't felt or seen, he is with us, just as he was with the children of Israel going through the Red Sea (see Psalm 77:19–20).

Dennis and Ginger dropped into bed around two in the morning. Then the phone rang. Back in Dallas, their eighteen-year-old daughter, Missy, was in critical condition, struck—hit-and-run—by a car while crossing the four-lane street that runs by the CFN campus where the family lived. I myself was living on campus at the time.

Dennis remembers, "As I hung up the phone, my mind was spinning. My wife and I immediately prayed. Feeling totally helpless, there was little we could do but turn to God and trust him to bring glory out of this situation. After reading Psalm 91, I slept peacefully the entire night without waking up. Ginger was not quite that fortunate."

Missy had been hit by a five-thousand-pound Cadillac. The driver had run a couple of red lights, going at speeds of up to fifty miles per hour. The impact threw Missy about thirty feet, causing severe head injuries. She had no heartbeat or any sign of breathing for seven minutes. Her pupils did not respond to light. The chief of campus security arrived at the scene within minutes and initially reported the incident as a D.O.A. (dead on arrival).

But Missy's miracle was just beginning. Immediately, prayer began at the scene of the accident, with many students gathering to pray around Missy's limp body. Word spread quickly, and intercession began all over campus. Students and staff members called friends, both in the United States and overseas, asking them to pray.

A knock came on our own door, reporting that Missy was probably dead. Jumping in the car with some faculty members, we rushed to the hospital to join others praying there.

The next morning when Dennis called from Argentina, the news was more encouraging. Now in intensive care, Missy's vital signs were stable; she was conscious, though unable to see clearly. An MRI and X-rays showed that nothing was broken; there were no injured organs and no blood clots in her head or body.

Dennis felt strongly that he was to finish his week in Argentina. A hard decision, I know, for parents so far away. But Missy's maternal grandparents were with her, and they had lots of praying friends in Dallas. Missy still had pain from a mild concussion, but her sight was improving.

On Wednesday—three days after the accident—she was released from the hospital. The following Saturday, on crutches, her arms and legs still covered with bruises, she was at the airport to meet her parents. The following Monday she went back to school, still supported by crutches. She was disappointed that she couldn't play any of the sports she loved during the rest of her senior year in high school. But her accident had not hindered her academically; she graduated sixth from the top of her class.

Missy had a supernatural touch from God and came away from her accident with only a limp, which lasted for several months. This incident serves as a definite reminder of God's loving care and protection for his children—the very message her dad was sharing in Argentina the evening the accident occurred.

Missy's mother says, "God takes care of his children! We tell our three children that all the time. Missy's miraculous healing is just another confirmation."

I strongly agree with Jamie Buckingham, who wrote: "God feels our sorrows, our misery, our anxiety. He weeps with us. He also feels our elation, our joy, our relief—and He laughs with us. The greatest thing Jesus taught us about God is that He is a God who cares."[2]

Whatever you are going through—know that he cares!

HIT BY A TRAIN

Palm Sunday, April 9, 1995, 6:55 A.M. Danny and Mary Kahler knew their seventeen-year-old son, Nathan, had not come home from a party after the high school prom. They tried not to worry about it as they reached for their morning coffee. Then the shrill buzz of Danny's rescue pager went off abruptly.

Danny was the rescue captain for the ambulance service in their small town of Fairmont, Nebraska. A train had hit a car at the Rose Avenue crossing. Nathan—could it be his car? Danny tried to push the frightful thought aside. He ran out the door while Mary began to pray, asking God to spare the life of whoever it was.

Danny rushed to the fire station, started the ambulance, and told his partner they did not have time to get their turnout gear; he had a gut feeling—an inner knowing—they were going to rescue his son. Danny drove the ambulance four blocks, to within sight of the intersection. Sure enough, there was Nathan's car, knocked onto the side-track by the impact of the train. Danny had helped extri-cate ten people from car-train accidents in the past five years. Five had been fatalities; the others had suffered per-manent disabilities. Now his son was a possible fatality. Why hadn't the village board voted to close down this crossing—as the railroad had suggested?

He did not want to go any closer to the wreckage. His partner shifted to the driver's seat and drove over to Nathan's car by himself. *How will I tell Mary that it was Nathan?* Danny wondered, anticipating the worst. He prayed silently. When the fire truck arrived, Danny told the chief they would need a piece of rescue equipment known as the "jaws of life" to pry Nathan out.

When his ambulance partner walked up to the window of Nathan's car, Danny heard him ask, "Are you okay?" Danny did not hear a response. But then he heard a second question: "Do you hurt anywhere else?" Nathan was respond-ing! Danny ran across the highway and right up to the car. One look told him his son was seriously injured—but alive.

As more volunteers arrived, Danny called Mary. "It's Nathan. Hit by a train. Wait at home until I can get there." Mary immediately called the prayer chain for her women's fellowship. Within a half hour prayer groups across Nebraska were alerted, joined soon by people from Denver to Detroit, praying for Nathan's life.

As soon as Nathan was in the ambulance, Danny went home. Mary's parents drove them the eight miles to the hospital. No one spoke during the drive. They were all praying.

It didn't take long for emergency room doctors to determine that Nathan needed a large hospital with a trauma center. As he was loaded into the ambulance for the trip to Lincoln, his vitals signs shut down. The Kahler's doc-tor rode in the ambulance with him and along the way administered emergency medical treatment that no doubt kept him alive. At the Lincoln hospital they learned one of his kidneys had "died" and both lungs were in trouble. His spleen was bleeding. Several vertebrae were fractured.

When the trauma surgeon asked Kahler's doctor why he had ridden with Nathan in the ambulance, he replied, "I have not seen a train accident victim live, and I wanted to see this boy live."

On Easter Sunday—exactly one week after the accident—Nathan came home from the hospital to recuperate. For weeks to come Mary heard from prayer intercessors, saying they had been praying for Nathan. Mary knows their prayers were answered.

Nathan had back pain for a while, and his recovery would take time. He lost one kidney, but otherwise his injuries were not permanent disabilities. He graduated a year later, happy to be alive.

Danny reports that after *this* accident, the railroad crossing was closed. It seems Nathan had fallen asleep at the wheel. The train engineer said his six hundred ton machine was going fifty-five miles an hour when it hit Nathan's car on the passenger side. How could one possibly survive such an impact? The entire Kahler family recognized God's hand of protection in sparing Nathan's life, especially because his car had been totally destroyed—except for the driver's seat. And there even the steering wheel tilt release still worked, enabling the rescue crew to get him out more easily.

When it comes to the "jaws of life," it seems as if there is nothing quite like our miracle-working God.

WHEN THE EARTH QUAKED

This next story is about two families in Guatemala when an earthquake hit in February 1976. One family was American, on a mission trip, the other Guatemalan. God's protection and safety for them was powerfully demonstrated.

Elizabeth and Floyd Alves and their family were spending their first night in the apartment above El Calvario
Church in Guatemala City. They had driven in that day
from San Antonio, Texas, with a fifteen passenger van full
of food, clothing, and blankets for these church members.
Beth was scheduled to speak at a conference in Guatemala
City. She picks up the story:

We had first been assigned to a little guest house out in
the country belonging to some missionaries. After five days
of travel in the van, the cottage looked so welcome, and we
rested a bit. Then around six that evening, I told Floyd, "I
feel an urgency for us to go back to Guatemala City now. I'm
sure we can spend the night in the apartment above the
church." I thought that if we waited until the next day, we
might be delayed at various checkpoints. Since I was scheduled to speak at a conference, I did not want to be late.

So we drove to Guatemala City. Now it was three in
the morning. I read again a verse in Isaiah 41, "Do not fear,
for I am with you." I had been lying in bed since midnight
meditating on this Scripture about coastlands being afraid,
the ends of the earth trembling, and neighbors helping
neighbors:

> The islands have seen it and fear;
>   the ends of the earth tremble.
> They approach and come forward;
>   each helps the other
>   and says to his brother, "Be strong". . . .
> So do not fear, for I am with you;
>   do not be dismayed, for I am your God.
> I will strengthen you and help you.
>
> ISAIAH 41:5–6, 10A

I looked at my watch—two minutes past three. The
dog on the roof by our window let out a mournful howl.
Other animals down the road were wailing. I wondered what
was causing such an awful commotion.

Then, without warning, our bed suddenly flipped up in the air and bounced back down to the floor with great force, as though a powerful hand was pushing it. Floyd and I prayed. It was the only thing we knew to do. But the earth kept trembling.

When I raised myself out of the bed, I fell against the wall, breaking my watch. "I've got to see about our girls. I'm going after them," I called to Floyd as I stumbled, half falling, toward their bedroom.

"Señor, get out. Pastor says for your family to get out of this building. Hurry! Hurry!" a young boy standing at our front door shouted at us. I grabbed my Bible and under-clothes and made a dash for the stairs, our girls in toe. We made our way down the stairs, which were already sepa-rating from the building.

The sky was a brilliant glow, orange-red in color with yellow clouds puffing across the horizon. Was all the earth on fire? "Do not fear," flashed before my mind once again. I was amazed at the inner peace I felt as we crawled into the van for safety.

The massive earthquake that racked Guatemala at 7.6 on the Richter scale at 3:02 A.M. on February 4, 1976, lasted only thirty seconds. When all the tremors subsided, more than three hundred towns had been destroyed and more than one million people were homeless. An estimated sev-enty-seven thousand were injured and twenty-three thou-sand were killed. Of course, I didn't know the extent of the damage as we sat in the van huddled between blankets.

Thankful to God for the safety of our family, I thought back over the events that had led us to this spot—arriving just in time to be in one of the worst calamities to hit this small Latin American country. We had been scheduled to bring the van to Guatemala City two months earlier, but the van had not come to the dealer from the factory.

When we received news the van was finally on its way, we prepared to leave, asking our pastor and congregation in

Texas to pray for us, our trip, and our mission. We started packing the van for our long drive. People from our church kept arriving at our home with blankets, sheets, coats, and jackets, wanting us to deliver them to needy Guatemalans. All the time I thought the donated items slightly inappropriate. Didn't Guatemala have a mild climate? Why would people need blankets?

I was also puzzled by the abundance of canned goods donated for us to take. And just before we left, I threw six gallons of water into the van. Allen, our teenage passenger, also brought six gallons. Why? I wondered. Surely we didn't need that much water.

The first major earthquake shock had covered 3,530 square miles, and Guatemala had been, in essence, ripped in two. We felt numerous tremors following the first massive quakes.

Floyd and I helped in whatever way we could. Over the next seven days we bedded down with our family each night in the van, happy to call it "home." Though our conference was cancelled, we stayed to assist the injured and homeless. Distributing blankets and canned foods, we realized why God had directed our church members to send so much in our van. Our extra water was desperately needed too.

When Floyd drove out into the country to check on the missionary family who had initially offered us their cottage, he saw that a cement post had fallen across the beds where our family would have been sleeping. God had certainly directed us to go into Guatemala City instead of staying there that night.

We saw neighbor helping neighbor, just as I had read in Isaiah 41 only minutes before the big quake. People distributed food. Some buried bodies. It was as if everyone seemed to have a specific task, a God-given calling.

Two days later, just as relief and rescue operations were well underway, a second strong quake hit, touching off a new wave of panic. More than one hundred tremors were felt in Guatemala City, and property damage to this city of one and a half million people was tremendous. Approximately fifty-eight thousand homes were destroyed. But the small towns were hit even harder. The pastor who had invited me to speak at the conference had 160 mission churches; hundreds of Christians had come into the city for the conference. Many of these village people's lives were saved because they were in the city, out of their hometowns.

After seven days of helping all we could, we returned to San Antonio, where Floyd assisted in further relief efforts by sending to Guatemala four truckloads of building supplies and a dump truck.

Of course, many stories have come out of this Guatemalan earthquake, but I choose the story of one other family, Regina and Santiago De Broll and their four children, who attended the El Calvario Church. Four months before the earthquake a Guatemalan Christian had a vision of such a disaster hitting the country, resulting in many deaths. When she submitted her vision—including an exact date and time—to the pastors for their discernment, they prayed, fasted, and sought God's direction. Afterwards they agreed it was indeed a warning from God.

"Our pastor told our congregation a big earthquake was coming, and he advised us to be prepared by the end of January," said Regina. "He did not tell us the day, only to have supplies ready. From his preaching we could tell we had better be sure that we had no unconfessed sin in our lives and that we should keep our relationship with the Lord right. He kept saying, 'Don't be afraid. God will take care of his children.'"

Regina had been a Christian only three years, but she believed the report and prepared her children and her maids. They practiced how to evacuate their home. They stored up water, juices, candles, rice, beans, and other food stuffs.

"My husband, Santiago, heard the same message in church as I did, but he did not believe it. A lot of people did not take seriously the warning to prepare. When one of my close friends tried to caution her friends and family, they called her crazy. But her entire family came to the Lord after the earthquake," Regina continued.

When she heard the earthquake hit, Regina was glad she had believed God's warning and was ready. She continues her story:

I felt the greatness and awesomeness of God's power to keep us safe.

When the earthquake hit, it was almost comical because my husband got tangled up in the sheets in his hurry to get outside. Our living quarters were on the second floor, so I made my way through broken glass to get my daughters while my husband got our sons out. The maids took a different route to safety.

Once outside, we went as far from our house as we could, which happened to be our garden. There we knelt, prayed, and sang until daybreak. We were cold and shivering. I had never seen my husband pray so long and so hard. He even gave the house to the Lord and cried out for mercy.

We cooked outdoors over a coal burning stove for the next two weeks and slept in our cars at night. My husband had to go into work in the daytime; my maids and I ran into the house and brought out what we could, little by little. Eventually the tremors stopped, and we could begin cleaning up the inside of the house.

After the earthquake, many non-Christians accepted the Lord, just as the Philippian jailer did when the earthquake hit the prison in which Paul was held. Many in Guatemala knew their Christian friends had been practicing how to evacuate from their homes and had stored necessary emergency supplies. They had heard the warning and accepted it as from God, and they were able to share with those who were not prepared.

Afterwards I felt a bit ashamed that I had not warned any of my non-Christian friends that an earthquake was coming.

Regina and her family had trusted God as their Protector and Deliverer. In the day of trouble, God sheltered her family and kept them safe.

As horrible as some "natural disasters" are, if you dig for "the rest of the story," you can usually find some life-changing results. Recall the story about Paul and Silas, badly beaten, fastened in stocks, and thrown into prison in Philippi? At midnight as the two were praying and singing, an earthquake shook the foundations of the prison, loosing their chains and opening the doors.

Thinking that the prisoners had escaped, the jailer was ready to kill himself. "Don't harm yourself," Paul assured him. "We are all here" (Acts 16:28). That day the jailer and his whole household came to believe in Paul's God. Herbert Lockyer notes: "God sent the earthquake, His servants were supernaturally delivered, and the jailer was supernaturally saved."[3]

Today we still can look to God as our Protector, our strong Rock of defense, who is an ever-present help in trouble (see Psalm 46).

Our next chapter will encourage you to hang on when you need a miracle—and never give up.

Praying the Scriptures
GOD OUR PROTECTOR AND DELIVERER

God is our refuge and strength, an ever-present help in trouble.

PSALM 46:1

The LORD is my rock, my fortress and my deliverer; my God is my rock, in whom I take refuge. He is my shield and the horn of my salvation, my stronghold.

PSALM 18:2

The LORD will keep you from all harm—he will watch over your life; the LORD will watch over your coming and going both now and forevermore.

PSALM 121:7–8

My people will live in peaceful dwelling places, in secure homes, in undisturbed places of rest.

ISAIAH 32:18

Even though I walk through the valley of the shadow of death, I will fear no evil, for you are with me; your rod and your staff, they comfort me.

PSALM 23:4

I lift up my eyes to the hills—where does my help come from? My help comes from the LORD, the Maker of heaven and earth.

PSALM 121:1–2

Believe me [Jesus] when I say that I am in the Father and the Father is in me; or at least believe on the evidence of the miracles themselves.

JOHN 14:11

PART EIGHT

Never Give Up on Your Miracle

*Let us hold unswervingly to the hope we pro-
fess, for he who promised is faithful.*

HEBREWS 10:23

When once I am persuaded that a thing is right
and for the glory of God, I go on praying for it
until the answer comes. George Müller never
gives up!

GEORGE MÜLLER

I have a challenge, written by the great missionary William Carey, posted above my computer. It's a motto I try to apply in my life.

Expect great things from God.
Attempt great things for God.

When I crawl into bed at night, my eyes are drawn to a wall plaque given me by my son, with Jesus' familiar quotation on it: "With God all things are possible" (Matthew 19:26). Each night I am reminded that nothing facing me is too big for my God—even if it looks too big to me.

I think of the children of Israel as they were heading toward the Promised Land. God had answered prayer after prayer, providing for their needs. Camped at Kadesh Barnea, they sent twelve spies, who went into the Promised Land to check out the region. Ten of the twelve came back with a negative report: "We can't attack those people; they are stronger than we are. . . . All the people we saw there are of great size. . . . We seemed like grasshoppers in our own eyes, and we looked the same to them" (Numbers 13:31–33).

The Israelite people—God's own chosen ones—believed the majority report, not God's word to them. As a result, the generation that came out of Egypt did not enter the Promised Land except for the two spies who believed that God would give them the land as he had promised—Caleb and Joshua (see Numbers 14:26–38).

At the beginning of this book we asked the question, "How do you pray for a miracle?" We mentioned some of the important ingredients—notably, to believe and have faith in the God who created us.

One key thread running through the stories of the people I have written about in this book is that they chose to believe God regardless of a doctor's hopeless reports, regardless of the danger they were in, regardless of lost things and loved ones, regardless of broken relationships. When they had a promise from God, they clung to it! They believed—and they said so with their mouths. Yes, there were times when some wavered, facing the possibility that death was imminent. Yet they cried out the name of Jesus and asked his help when they felt most helpless.

And yes, sometimes miracles occur even when we have not even asked for them or believed they were possible. Such miracles happen just because God loves us and wills them so.

When we experience a miracle, I believe God wants us to share it with others so that he gets the attention, the credit, the honor. How can you strengthen the faith of someone who needs a miracle? In humility share the story of your own miracle. I love Sandy Horn's story (see Part 6). She was healed of cancer in five areas in her body. You may recall she felt God asking her to return home and tell others how much God had done for her. As a result, her husband became a believer.

Jesus was known as the Miracle-Worker, but not for his own gain or honor. He always pointed the healed and delivered ones and their spectators to the heavenly Father. Of Jesus' miracles Jamie Buckingham says,

> It was never for His own benefit. He never changed a camel into a Cadillac. He never even changed the rocks into bread so He could have something to eat. The night He was arrested He could have called the angels to protect Him from the soldiers. Instead, He submitted Himself to God's higher plan— the plan of the cross. His miracles were for one purpose only—for the glory of God.[1]

And so ought ours to be.

Let's look in this final chapter at a few tenacious prayers—people who would not give up praying for the miracle they wanted.

A "SMALL" REQUEST

Elizabeth, a single mom with three children, had a specific request she repeatedly presented before God. She was in love with Daniel, a chief petty officer in the U.S. Navy. While he was in the thick of the battle in the Pacific during World War II, she kept writing him, saying she would see him on his birthday.

Not wanting her to hope in vain, Daniel wrote back in every letter, "Under the circumstances of this war, I don't see how I can possibly see you by April 17." But every night Betty prayed for his safety and thanked God in advance that Daniel would be with her for his birthday.

She began to count the days, fully expecting God to answer her prayers. Sure enough, he arrived in Houston on his birthday—April 17, 1945—and fell into the arms of his beloved Betty. The war ended in August when Japan surrendered. Daniel and Betty married soon thereafter.

I know this story well, because I heard it often enough from my Uncle D. C. and Aunt Betty Lammon. A family miracle!

Aunt Betty's prayer request and God's response may seem inconsequential when compared to the next story of a man whose faith has become legendary.

FIFTY THOUSAND ANSWERED PRAYERS

George Müller, known for feeding and housing thousands of orphans in Bristol, England, in the nineteenth century, estimated God answered more than fifty thousand of his prayers—usually on the day he asked. In his diary, he wrote, "God has never failed me! For nearly seventy years every need in connection with this work has been supplied. All has come in answer to believing prayer."

Once when he was crossing the Atlantic for a speaking engagement in Canada, dense fog settled in. The ship could not move for danger of colliding with another vessel. Müller knelt beside the captain and prayed, asking God to lift the fog. As they walked out on the deck, the captain's face expressed astonishment. The fog had completely lifted, and Müller reached Canada on time. Believing prayer was what this great saint always practiced.

Some of his prayers were not answered so quickly, of course. He prayed for fifty-two years that two men, sons of a friend of his, might know Jesus. His prayer was answered shortly after his death when both became Christians—one, in fact, at Müller's funeral. Müller said that when he was persuaded something was for the glory of God, he never gave up praying until the answer came![2]

The prayers of a righteous person are powerful and effective. As the letter of James says, "The earnest (heartfelt, continued) prayer of a righteous man makes tremendous power available—dynamic in its working" (James 5:16 AMPLIFIED). Pastor Dutch Sheets comments on this verse:

> Don't think you are releasing enough power to accomplish the miraculous by sporadic or casual praying. You are not! You must release the power of God inside of you on a consistent basis. . . . This verse is telling us, "A prayer of a righteous person is able to do much as it—the prayer—operates." Our prayers go to work.[3]

Our next story helps illustrate this.

FAITH IN GOD'S ABILITY

When their teenage daughter experienced brain damage in an automobile accident, Rose and Grady Barton chose to believe God's word to them instead of all the negative and hopeless doctor reports. Rose tells the story:

Our daughter Rose Ann was a freshman in high school, an outstanding student scholastically. One day she was riding home with friends, laughing and relieved that her mid-term exams were behind her. Another car crossed over into their lane of traffic and hit the back passenger side of the car—right where Rose Ann was sitting. She suffered severe brain damage, both her lungs were punctured by broken ribs, and the upper right side of her body was crushed.

When we got to the hospital, doctors were reluctant to let us see her. A minister friend who did get in came back with a report: "Now is the time to pray. She is dying. Two doctors and five nurses are working over her."

My husband, Grady, praying in the hall outside the intensive care unit, sensed what he believed was a word from God: "I'm going to raise her up; you will see it, and she will be completely healed." Twenty-five friends soon joined us in the hospital prayer chapel to pray for her.

I was kneeling near the front when God seemed to ask me a question: "What have we been talking about lately?"

"Miracles, Lord, miracles."

At that moment the words "he is able to keep that which I have committed unto him" dropped into my heart, and with the hearing of those words came a supernatural faith to believe for Rose Ann. At the time, I had no idea that those words were from 2 Timothy 1:12 (KJV)—the hearing of those words and the faith that dropped into my heart were as supernatural as Rose Ann's healing to me.

It took lots of *faith* to believe for a miracle. Rose Ann had so many tubes attached to her body and was still bleeding, and her face was so swollen that I hardly recognized my own daughter. Even though she was in a coma, her Daddy would quote Scriptures and I would talk to her as though she understood. We kept telling her God was healing her; we encouraged her with words, though we did not know if she was hearing us.

The doctors did not think Rose Ann would live the first seventy-two hours. If she did, they anticipated she would be in a vegetable-like state. One surgeon in particular wanted to "prepare" me to accept the fact that she would never be normal.

But we simply learned a new level of prayer. We listened to the doctors reports and then prayed directly against the prognosis. When she got an infection as they predicted, we called our friends to pray against that specific bacteria—and her condition turned around.

When her right side became paralyzed, doctors bored holes in her skull to relieve the pressure on her brain. She still remained paralyzed for over two weeks, but we kept praying. At one point when my husband was praying, he saw an image of a "dark cloud" on her brain, but he did not know what it meant.

After two weeks in a coma, Rose Ann woke up. We played Christian music and Scripture tapes almost constantly. She seemed to improve when we were with her, praying. At first she couldn't talk. But one day when she heard her grandfather on the phone, she answered back. We were thrilled. Through prayer her paralysis lessened; with minor physical therapy, she was able to use her body again.

Twenty-six days after the accident, Rose Ann came home. But she couldn't remember anything that had happened in the past few months. She couldn't even recall what she had just said to us or what she had eaten for breakfast. Grady now remembered the "dark cloud" on the side of her head he had seen while in prayer. Going into her room, he laid hands on her head and prayed. The next day her short-term memory was restored.

When she went back to school six weeks after the accident, she relearned much of the material that had been erased in her brain—all but math, a subject she had previously excelled in. She waited to take her final math exam after she had been tutored all summer. But tutoring did not help, for she still had no understanding of math problems.

But hadn't God told Grady in the hospital that Rose Ann would be healed? *Yes, God had promised. But she's not healed,* he said to himself. A new level of faith grew in him, like an expanding balloon, larger and larger.

One Thursday evening he took Rose Ann to a Bible study, where several other men joined him in praying for her *finished* healing. By morning, she received another God-given miracle: She could grasp math. She took the exam and passed with good grades. I know that only God can restore a brain, not a doctor.

It has been twenty-five years since Rose Ann was healed. She graduated from college *cum laude* and became a school teacher. Her parents credit her miracle to God, yes, but also to the persistent and specific prayers of friends who stood firm with them in their belief of God's miracle-working power.

A SOLDIER CRIES "HELP" IN THE NIGHT

Harry Ormsby of London, Kentucky, was only twenty years old when he returned to the States from Vietnam in June 1972. Transferred to an Army post in Colorado, he kept on drinking, partying, and smoking marijuana with his buddies. But he was miserable. He longed to stop his lifestyle, but he didn't know how. Then he had a supernatural encounter in the middle of the night. He tells his story:

After all the killing I had seen in Vietnam, I wondered if God even existed. If he did, I wasn't sure if I could know him. And yet during the five months after I got back to the States, an overwhelming desire was growing inside me to know God. I think someone somewhere was praying for me. I started praying a lot myself. And yet I kept on going out with the guys, smoking pot.

One night when I had been out late, living it up, I felt empty and dissatisfied. As I walked up the steps to my apartment, tears started falling down my cheeks. I paused on the landing halfway up and looked up at the dark sky. I suddenly found myself talking aloud to God. "If you don't do whatever you do to save people, to help them, I'm not going to make it. Do whatever you do," I stammered.

As I kept gazing at the dark sky, suddenly right before my eyes Jesus appeared on the cross. He had a very bloodied and swollen head; the skin on his cheeks looked as though his beard had been plucked out. His countenance was almost beyond recognition. I was in awe, yet frightened. My sins—every one I had ever done—seemed to be hanging on him.

I ducked my head down and started to cry. "Lord, forgive me. There is nothing I can do to pay you back. I am so sorry." I looked back up, and Jesus was no longer on the cross but directly in front of me, looking at me with great joy. His eyes said everything—love and forgiveness. When I acknowledged his presence, he smiled, reached out, and touched me on the forehead. Then he was gone.

I knew at that moment he forgave and loved me! Perhaps seeing a vision or revelation of Jesus is a miracle, and I don't treat it lightly. But to me the real miracle was the continuous way God changed my life, my attitudes, my actions, and my desires. His power came that night and touched me deeply. No more drinking. No more drugs. No more partying. In the more than twenty years I have followed him since that night, he has continued to change my heart. I have even had the opportunity to go to other countries to tell people about a loving and forgiving Savior.

Harry was desperate when he cried out to God: "Do whatever you do to save, to help people." Often we have to admit our own helplessness to experience our miracle.

MIRACULOUS RESUSCITATION

The Bible records incidents where God has empowered people even to bring the dead back to life. Reviewing some of the accounts may cause us to wonder if perhaps some of us give up on our miracle too soon.

Elijah and Elisha in the Old Testament each were instrumental in praying life back into a young man. Elijah's prayer went like this: "O LORD my God, let this boy's life return to him!" The Lord heard Elijah's cry, and the prophet gave the boy to his mother, saying "Look, your son is alive!" (see 1 Kings 17:21–23; cf. 2 Kings 4:34). What joy must have welled up in her heart.

Jesus restored the son of a widow when the mourners were on the way to bury him: "Young man, I say to you, get up!" (Luke 7:14). He called Lazarus, already dead four days and stinking, out of the tomb: "Lazarus, come out!" (John 11:43). Jesus had told Lazarus's sister Martha that if she *believed* he would perform this miracle, she would see the glory of God. Jesus also raised Jairus's dead daughter in the privacy of her home: "My child, get up" (Luke 8:54).

Peter knelt and prayed beside the cold body of Dorcas, a beloved disciple who had made garments for the poor. Dorcas was one of the seven resurrections, apart from Christ's, mentioned in the Bible.[4]

You may think it must have seemed easier to believe for such miracles in the early church than now. Yet reports from around the world indicate that such miracles are still happening. I'll give you a few examples, starting with one of which I have personal knowledge. Remember that Jesus said if his followers had faith in him, they would be able to do what he was doing, and even greater things—more miracles. He also said, "And I will do whatever you ask in my name, so that the Son may bring glory to the Father," he added (see John 14:12–13). He told his followers, "Heal the sick, raise the dead, cleanse those who have leprosy, drive out demons" (Matthew 10:8), giving us his permission and authority to do miracles in his name.

My friend Judy Ball is a North Carolina grandmother who believes that nothing is impossible for God. While babysitting her two small grandchildren, she *needed* a Scripture verse she had heard just the day before.

She tells her story:

When a missionary told our women's prayer group about an African baby raised from the dead, I said to myself, "I believe that." I wrote the Scripture she shared in the front of my Bible. "'For I have no pleasure in the death of one who dies,' says the Lord GOD. 'Therefore turn and live!'" (Ezekiel 18:32 NKJV).

The next day I was taking care of my eighteen-month-old grandson, Marshall, and his sister while their parents and my husband were in church. As I rocked Marshall, I suddenly realized that he was not breathing. I jumped to my feet, shaking him and yelling, "Marshall, Marshall."

I remembered the Scripture. Aloud I said, "I believe this. The Lord doesn't take pleasure in the death of this child. Turn and live. Live, Marshall, live."

Over and over I repeated the Scripture, walking with him from room to room. I continued to loudly proclaim it. I was praying continually that God would perform a miracle for my precious little grandson.

But still Marshall would not breathe. He was turning blue, and his little body was starting to curl up in my arms.

"Live, Marshall. Live," I said, holding him tight to my heart, then placing him up on my shoulder. "Turn and live."

I weaved my way throughout the house, room to room, pacing, repeating the Scripture. God's peace overtook me. As far as I could tell he was already dead, but I was going to use God's Word to revive him.

Finally, after at least fifteen minutes of carrying a lifeless little body around, affirming the Scriptures aloud, I took him off my shoulder to look once more at his bluish face. No difference. But then I saw his smallest finger wiggle ever so slightly. His eyelids fluttered, and my little grandson was coming alive.

My knees began to tremble. I phoned the church to get a message to Marshall's parents to come home. But by the time they arrived, he was walking around the room as normal as could be. He never again had another incident like this.

But one day, when he was six years old, Marshall and I were having a heart-to-heart talk. He began to describe heaven for me. As he did, I realized he must have visited there when he was eighteen months old as I walked with his limp body, battling with God's Word for him to live.

Some of what he told me was like reading the description of heaven from the book of Revelation—the glassy sea, the angels worshiping the Lord, the beauty of it all. "You would have loved the beautiful flowers, Me Maw," he said with great excitement. "Also the angels, who were big. They wore white robes with gold at the top. I liked the big swimming pool because I could see all the way to the bottom because it was clear as glass."

Judy Ball, an ordinary woman with great experience as an intercessor, operated in the gift of faith to believe that "the working of miracles" is still accessible to God's people today (see 1 Corinthians 12:9–10). This "gift of faith" should not be confused with presumption that God will grant a specific request; as I said in Part 1, our faith is in God, not in miracles. The gift of faith is a unique form of faith that *supernaturally* trusts God without doubt. Intercessors with this faith have stood against all odds to believe for and see God supernaturally heal.

Sometime after Judy prayed for her grandson, she got a phone call from a friend asking her to come pray for his critically ill wife before doctors transferred her to another hospital. When Judy arrived, she heard the doctor tell the woman's husband, "We aren't going to move your wife. We have done all we can. I am sorry, but she is at the point of death."

"Then you wouldn't mind if I prayed in the room where she is, would you?" Judy asked the doctor.

"Go right ahead," he replied.

Judy donned a hospital gown, mask, and gloves and entered the room. Placing her hands on the bed, very quietly she repeated the same Scripture, "Turn and live." In a few moments the nurse monitoring the patient's machines told her, "Whatever you are doing is working, keep doing it. Her vital signs are improving."

Judy kept praying and repeating Scriptures, then left. As a result, the patient continued her improvement until she was soon able to go home, well and healed.

THE CHILD IS NOT DEAD, JUST SLEEPING

Prakash, a crusade worker in Karnataka, India, looked at the lifeless body of his son and felt his heart collapse with grief.

Prakash had been out in the field, sharing the Gospel in the village of Madhugiri, when he received an urgent telegram from his wife. He rushed home and discovered that his son was nearly dead. They couldn't afford an ambulance, so Prakash and his wife boarded a crowded bus and began the long journey to a hospital in a neighboring city. On the way, their son's heart stopped beating. All the passengers on the bus gave him up for lost.

"I felt as if a big bolt of lightning had struck my heart," Prakash said. "My sorrow knew no bounds, and my wife was fully immersed in tears."

But, in the midst of the tragedy, faith filled his heart with renewed confidence and power. "The child is not dead, just sleeping," Prakash announced with a boldness that made the passengers on the bus laugh as if he were insane.

Prakash immediately knelt down in the aisle of the bus and prayed over the body of his son. Ten minutes into his prayer, a pulse returned to the child's body, and he opened his eyes.

The passengers were stunned. "Your God is truly great!" they said in amazement. "Tell us something about Him."

Rejoicing in God's miraculous answer to his prayers, Prakash shared the Gospel with a captive audience.[5]

WAITING SIX YEARS FOR HIS MIRACLE

Sometimes our miracle comes when we have clung tenaciously to only a thin thread of hope. Deep down we believe God can perform a miracle for us, but as time passes, we resign ourselves. We may even pray, "God, I can learn to live without my miracle; but if anywhere along the way, you want to do it, I'm ready." That was Randy's position for almost six years.

Randy Ostrander was demonstrating how to use a shoulder-building exercise equipment known as the LAT bar to his wife, Marsha, and daughter Jennifer at the city-owned health center. The exercise machine had a bar attached to a cable that went through two pulleys, then connected to the weights. Suddenly the cable snapped, whipping the bar across the back of Randy's neck.

On that day—February 24, 1989—the thirty-eight-year-old Palm Bay, Florida, pastor found his life forever changed. The accident left him with a concussion, herniated discs, and the inability to raise his hands over his head or to move his head around. An MRI showed that one of the three ruptured discs had severely injured his spinal cord.

A month later when he checked into John Hopkins Hospital in Baltimore for his first surgery, he could barely walk. After three surgeries, four of his cervical vertebrae were fused together as one bone. Physical therapy helped him move from a wheelchair to walking on a cane. He wore neck collars for support.

Even after surgery, he had only thirty percent movement in his neck—to the right or left. He could not see the ceiling, let alone the sky. He was taking eight medications. Some for pain, some muscle relaxers, some antiseizure medication. "I was almost like a zombie," he remembers. He had to resign his job because of his physical limitations.

People from around the world prayed for him. He received letters and phone calls to reassure him: "Randy, God is going to heal you." Every time he went to a church service, it seemed as if someone would come up and pray for his healing. But he did not get healed.

Medical bills ate so deeply into their family finances they were about to lose their home. Friends pitched in and paid off his second mortgage—over twenty-four thousand dollars. Twenty men from area churches roofed the house.

Six years passed. Randy's question was, "How can God use me now?"

Then in January 1995 a series of renewal services began at the Melbourne Tabernacle Church, where Randy had once been an associate pastor. He had already attended two of the services and the visiting speaker, Randy Clark, had prayed for his healing. After services on the third night, a family friend whispered in his ear. "Randy, this is your night to be healed. Would you receive prayer?"

At first Randy thought, "I've been prayed for already twice this week, and it didn't work. But I won't turn down prayer."

Fifty people gathered around Randy to pray that night. He sat in a chair so he wouldn't lose his balance and injure his neck. Marsha and their sixteen-year-old son, Jamie, joined in the prayer. Randy Clark started praying, calling out all of Randy's symptoms: headache, pain in the neck, neurological damage. . . .

Then he asked, "Randy, do you feel anything different?"

"Yes, my headache just left."

As the twenty-minute prayer continued, each symptom Pastor Clark mentioned subsided. Jamie, a tough football player, began to sob. For days he had been asking God to give his dad a new neck.

Randy describes the night of his instant healing as "an electric moment." "I walked out able to look at the sky, moving my neck. We stayed up until three in the morning, calling our family and friends to tell them the good news."

Randy immediately quit taking all his medications except the one for seizures—which has to be eased off slowly.

One of his doctors, who became a Christian while treating Randy, compared his MRIs before and after the night of his prayer for healing. "There is no anatomical way you can move your head like you do. I have no other word to describe it, other than the word miracle."

Randy said later, "We never gave up on a miracle—Marsha and I—but we decided if God didn't heal me completely, we were still going to give him glory and see how he could use us. We are still getting used to our miracle. When something like this happens to you—a flat-out miracle—after six years, you cannot deny it really happened."

Walking even without a cane and being able to gaze at the sky seems like such little things to some, but not to Randy and Marsha Ostrander. God has used Randy to pray for others to receive healing. He has big faith now to know that you should never give up on your miracle.

YOU CAN BE SOMEONE ELSE'S MIRACLE

Sometimes God uses us as the catalyst for a miracle in someone else's life. True, on some occasions we know we are God's instruments; as we have seen in this book, our role is our prayer. Bible scholars indicate that half of the detailed healings in the gospels resulted from prayers of friends. But on other occasions we are sent as an answer to someone else's prayer.

I remember a clear brisk winter in Florida many years ago. Linda, a young reporter for the newspaper I worked on, was going through a painful, unwanted divorce. I would notice her crying at her desk. I wanted to be her friend, but we did not live in the same community. And honestly, I did not know how to reach out.

One evening I got a babysitter and took Linda out to eat. As we were about to leave in our separate cars, I called out, "Linda, I just remembered, today is February 14. Happy Valentine's. I love you."

"What did you say?" she asked, surprise in her voice.

"I love you," I repeated.

"Really? No woman outside my family has ever said she loved me. . . . I feel so unlovable right now."

"Well, with God's help you are going to make it through the pain. Jesus loves you, too."

Soon afterwards she moved to another state. She eventually remarried and had a son. But every Valentine's Day for ten years I received a beautiful card in the mail, always signed, "I love you, too. Linda."

Some twenty-four years after our initial Valentine's dinner, when I was traveling near her city, we arranged for a short visit. "You were a heaven-sent miracle to me that Valentine's night," she said. "Because you said you loved me, I had hope."

How easy it is to be a miracle in someone's life if we are sensitive to their hurts.

As you wait for, pray for, your own miracle, do not close yourself to God-given opportunities to be a miracle for someone else.

THE POWER OF PERSISTENT PRAYER

Some of us may even provide the prayer power needed for a miracle in the life of someone we don't know personally. I conclude this book with a story from my own pastor,

Dutch Sheets, who was once a catalyst for a remarkable miracle in the life of a woman who was a virtual stranger to him.

Pastor Sheets had agreed to pray for an extremely ill girl—he calls her Diane—at the request and insistence of her sister. When he entered upon this prayer journey, he had no idea that for more than a year Diane had been comatose with a tracheostomy in her throat and a feeding tube in her stomach. The outer layer of her brain, the doctors said, had been destroyed by a virus, and every part of it was covered with infection. They gave her no hope.

But Dutch prayed and believed he had a word from God that she would be restored. His persistent prayer for her—sixty to seventy times in the course of the next year as he stood beside her bed—illustrates persevering believing prayer. When he began, he never expected to spend three to four hours of his life each week going to pray for her. He never expected to be so intimidated at times or so bold at times, and he never thought it would take so long for healing to come.

One day Pastor Sheets received a call from a family member to say that Diane had taken a turn for the worse and the doctors expected her to die soon. Dutch rushed again to her side to pray. He tells about it in his book *Intercessory Prayer*:

> Knowing that comatose people can often hear and understand everything that is happening around them, I had spoken much to her. As we later learned, because of the damage to her brain Diane was not hearing me. But this Wednesday afternoon, I spoke to her as usual.
>
> "This nightmare is almost over," I said with tears streaming down my face. "Nothing can keep us from receiving our miracle. Nothing!" And as I exited the hospital weeping, I remember saying to myself again, "Nothing can keep us from our miracle. Nothing!"
>
> This was not just a strong hope I had at this point but a great faith. I had turned to God many times

throughout the course of that year, asking him if he had really sent me to this little girl. Each time I received his assurance: "I sent you. Don't quit."

My persistence was rewarded when, three days after visiting her in the hospital, Diane woke up with full restoration to her brain. News about the miracle spread everywhere.

Every hour and every tear I had invested became worth the wait when I saw Diane awake and heard her speak the words, "Praise the Lord."[6]

Yes, God restored Diane. He healed her brain. The newspaper in the city where she lived carried a headline "Woman Awake, Alive, Healthy After Two Years in a Coma."

Dutch Sheets often says, "I've learned that no one is born a prayer hero. They are shaped and refined on the practice field of life.

Many of us say with Pastor Sheets that we are still learning.

THANK HIM FOR YOUR MIRACLE

Testimonies of biblical and contemporary miracles prove wrong the skeptics who say miracles don't happen. Not all are momentous, of course. Nor are all immediate. But all of God's miracles are sent with his grace and for his glory.

You have had a few miracles in your life, I am sure. Just jar your memory a bit—and stop to thank God for intervening when you needed him most.

And yes, expect even more:

in your family . . .
at your workplace . . .
at your school . . .
in your neighborhood . . .

in your church . . .
in any crisis . . .
in everyday humdrum activities.

Why not start your own personal diary and record all the miracles God has done for you as you have prayed?

I end this book where I began it, with the premise that prayer is a catalyst for miracles.

Miracles happen when you pray!

Praying the Scriptures
HE WHO PROMISED IS FAITHFUL

No eye has seen, no ear has heard, no mind has conceived what God has prepared for those who love him.

1 CORINTHIANS 2:9B

Everything is possible for him who believes.

MARK 9:23B

I will remember the deeds of the LORD; yes, I will remember your miracles of long ago.

PSALM 77:11

Then Jesus answered, "Woman, you have great faith! Your request is granted." And her daughter was healed from that very hour.

MATTHEW 15:28

Now faith is being sure of what we hope for and certain of what we do not see.

HEBREWS 11:1

And without faith it is impossible to please God, because anyone who comes to him must believe that he exists and that he rewards those who earnestly seek him.

HEBREWS 11:6

If any of you lacks wisdom, he should ask God, who gives generously to all without finding fault, and it will be given to him. But when he asks, he must believe and not doubt, because he who doubts is like a wave of the seas, blown and tossed by the wind.

JAMES 1:5–6

Do not neglect to show hospitality to strangers, for by this some have entertained angels without knowing it.

HEBREWS 13:2 (NASB)

NOTES

PART ONE: PRAYING FOR A MIRACLE

1. C. Peter Wagner, *Confronting The Powers* (Ventura, Calif.: Regal Books, 1996), 23.

2. *Webster's New World Encyclopedia* (New York: Prentice Hall, 1993), 704.

3. Jamie Buckingham, *Miracle Power* (Ann Arbor, Mich.: Servant Publications, 1988), 9–10.

4. C. Peter Wagner, *Confronting The Powers*, 23.

5. Corrie ten Boom, *Not Good If Detached* (Fort Washington, Penn.: Christian Literature Crusade, 1973), 94–95; used with permission.

PART TWO: MIRACLES OF PROVISION

1. From an article by Religion News Service, © 1994; used by permission of RNS and of General Charles Krulak, Commandant of United States Marine Corps.

2. Christine Aroney-Sine, *Confessions of a Seasick Doctor* (Grand Rapids: Zondervan, 1966), 54–55; used by permission.

3. Quin Sherrer, "The Christmas Gift," *Christian Life* (December 1981), 22–23; used with permission of Strang Communication, Lake Mary, Fla.

PART THREE: MIRACLES OF THE HEART

1. Adapted from "Shattered and Reborn," by Hilda Forehand, as told to Quin Sherrer, *Charisma Magazine* (May 1985), 40–43; used with permission of Strang Communication.

2. Adapted from "The Song That Changed," by Quin Sherrer, *Aglow Magazine* (Lynnwood, Wash.: Aglow Publications, 1985), 15–18; used with permission.

PART FOUR: MIRACLES OF LOST AND FOUND

1. Adapted from "Something Vital Was Missing," by Ann Fraser as told to Quin Sherrer, *Aglow Magazine* (Lynnwood, Wash.: Aglow Publications, Winter, 1977), 12–15; used with permission.

PART FIVE: MIRACLES OF ANGELIC INTERVENTION

1. Ann Spangler, *An Angel a Day* (Grand Rapids: Zondervan, 1994), 16.

2. Billy Graham, *Angels, God's Secret Agents* (Dallas: Word, 1986), 20

3. See his comment in *The Spirit-Filled Life Bible* (Nashville: Thomas Nelson, 1991), 539.

4. Billy Graham, *Angels, God's Secret Agents*, 65, 67.

PART SIX: MIRACLES OF HEALING

1. Adapted from Bill Lance as told to Quin Sherrer, "Healed of Leukemia," *Charisma Magazine* (September 1984), 29–31; used with permission of Strang Communication.

2. Dutch Sheets, *Intercessory Prayer: How God Can Use Your Prayers to Move Heaven and Earth* (Ventura, Calif.: Regal Books, 1996), 103–4; used by permission.

3. Adapted from "His Body Broken for Me," by Peggy Davis as told to Quin Sherrer, *Aglow Magazine* (Lynnwood, Wash.: Aglow Publications, Spring 1975), 17–18; used with permission.

4. Adapted from "When No One Else Believed," by Sandy Horn as told to Quin Sherrer, *Aglow Magazine* (Lynnwood, Wash.: Aglow Publications, Spring 1974), 13–15; used with permission.

PART SEVEN: MIRACLES OF PROTECTION

1. Based on "Missy's Miracle," by CFNI President Dennis Lindsay, *Christ for the Nations Magazine* (March 1993), 4–5; used with permission.

2. Jamie Buckingham, *Miracle Power* (Ann Arbor, Mich.: Servant Publications, 1988), 206.

3. Herbert Lockyer, *All the Miracles of the Bible* (Grand Rapids: Zondervan, 1961), 286.

PART EIGHT: NEVER GIVE UP ON YOUR MIRACLE

1. Jamie Buckingham, *Miracle Power* (Ann Arbor, Mich.: Servant Publications, 1988), 40.

2. Roger Steer, *George Müller, Delighted in God* (Wheaton, Ill.: Harold Shaw, 1975), 310.

3. Dutch Sheets, *Intercessory Prayer: How God Can Use Your Prayer to Move Heaven and Earth* (Ventura, Calif.: Regal Books, 1996), 208; used by permission.

4. See Herbert Lockyer, *All the Miracles of the Bible* (Grand Rapids: Zondervan, 1961), 275.

5. *Every Home For Christ Newsletter*, Dick Eastman, president (Colorado Springs, Colo., January, 1995); used with permission.

6. Dutch Sheets, *Intercessory Prayer*, 16–18; used by permission.